Evangelizing

EVANGELIZING TODAY'S DOMESTIC CHURCHES

A Theological and Pastoral Approach to the Family

Rev. Robert J. Hater, Ph.D.

Our Sunday Visitor
Huntington, Indiana

Nihil Obstat
Msgr. Michael Heintz, Ph.D.
Censor Librorum

Imprimatur
✠ Kevin C. Rhoades
Bishop of Fort Wayne-South Bend
May 31, 2022

The *Nihil Obstat* and *Imprimatur* are official declarations that a book is free from doctrinal or moral error. It is not implied that those who have granted the *Nihil Obstat* and *Imprimatur* agree with the contents, opinions, or statements expressed.

Our Sunday Visitor Publishing Division
Our Sunday Visitor, Inc.
200 Noll Plaza
Huntington, IN 46750
www.osv.com
1-800-348-2440

ISBN: 978-1-68192-927-9 (Inventory No. T2670)
1. RELIGION—Christian Ministry—Pastoral Resources.
2. RELIGION—Christian Life—Family.
3. RELIGION—Christianity—Catholic.

eISBN: 978-1-68192-928-6
LCCN: 2022942071

Cover design and Interior design: Amanda Falk
Cover art and Interior art: AdobeStock

Printed in the United States of America

I dedicate this book to my parents, Stanley and Olivia Hater; to my sisters, Mary Ann Haubner and Joan Kohl; and to my deceased brother, Thomas Hater. Dad and Mom, thanks for setting the climate for our domestic church through your love and dedication to our Catholic Faith.

I also dedicate this book to Sr. Judy Gradel, RSM and to the sisters and staff of Mercy McAuley Convent in Cincinnati, Ohio. After I was hit by a car and suffered serious injuries, including a broken hip and other bodily trauma, in May 2019, they invited me to stay and recuperate in the guest room with their retirement community. Their care, concern, and support provided me with the incentive to go on after my serious injuries. I will be forever grateful to them for the faith, love, and inspiration that I witnessed in this wonderful Christian community.

CONTENTS

Foreword

As a priest and now as a young bishop, I am always amazed at how God brings people into our lives who somehow inspire us to think and, at the same time, encourage us to be better, even if it means looking at things differently. Five years ago, I met Fr. Robert Hater in my role as editor for *The Priest* magazine, which is published by OSV. I will never forget one of the nuggets of pastoral advice he offered to priests in one of his many articles. He mentioned that we as priests need to live from the inside out. In other words, we cannot allow external events to sway us from the mission with which we are charged.

Although I have never personally met Father Hater face-to-face, I have corresponded with him and even have had a few telephone conversations involving content that he has produced from time to time for *The Priest* magazine. I have found his reflections to be pastoral, timely, and poignant. His contributions to the Church have been prolific and not limited solely to priests or even his own Archdiocese of Cincinnati. In short, Father Hater has contributed much to the work of faith formation in the life of the Church. This newly published book is but another way for him to share his theological and pastoral insights for the good of the Church.

I am both humbled and honored by Father Hater's request to write this foreword. Father Hater is a priest of over sixty years. His witness and wisdom have left an indelible mark on the life of the Church. It is evident from the stories contained in this book that Father Hater's love for Jesus and the Church, not to mention his vocation to the priesthood, grew from his experience in the domestic church of his family. How fitting that he dedicates this work to his dear parents and family, who in so many ways modeled what it means to be a domestic church.

When most people think about their experience of Church, what typically comes to mind is the parish. In his apostolic exhortation, *Evangelii Guadium*, Pope Francis speaks about the parish. He writes:

> The parish is not an outdated institution; precisely because it possesses great flexibility, it can assume quite different contours depending on the openness and missionary creativity of the pastor and the community. While certainly not the only institution which evangelizes, if the parish proves capable of self-renewal and constant adaptivity, it continues to be "the Church living in the midst of the homes of her sons and daughters." This presumes that it really is in contact with the homes and the lives of its people, and does not become a useless structure out of touch with people or a self-absorbed group made up of a chosen few. … We must admit, though, that the call to review and renew our parishes has not yet sufficed to bring them nearer to

people, to make them environments of living communion and participation, and to make them completely mission-oriented.[1]

Father Hater's work toward revitalizing domestic churches is an opportunity for pastors, parochial vicars, and pastoral ministers and teams to become closer to God's people, most especially those who form the domestic church, and to make parishes stronger and more vibrant.

At a time which is best described by Father Hater as a crossroads and crisis filled with many challenges, these reflections demonstrate a significant shift in focus for faith formation in the life of the Church. According to Father Hater there is much that pastors can glean from the early Church when it comes to the domestic church. The result is not necessarily new ministries, programs, or structures but "refocusing existing parish ministries in light of the family." As Father Hater addresses new directions in family outreach, he quotes Pope Francis in *Amoris Laetitia*: "Don't get bogged down in your own limited ideas and opinions, but be prepared to change or expand them."[2]

In these pages, Father Hater presents a solid strategy for faith formation centered around the family. He invites parishes and their leadership to assist families in the fourfold dynamic envisioned by Pope Francis; namely, welcome, accompaniment, discernment, and integration. Father Hater digs deeply into developing a theology of the domestic church.

Ever the man of hope, Father Hater offers opportunities in these challenging times. Father Hater frames these opportunities in terms of calls, all of which help to form and strengthen the domestic church that no doubt could enhance the parish. As always, there are no quick fixes to this effort. It is hard work in a challenging time for any parish. In fact, Father Hater writes, "No magic formula exists to answer the internal challenges that parishes face. Pastors need to rely on the wisdom given by the Holy Spirit, focus on the needs of the Catholic community, and stress the importance of the parish in its relationship with the domestic church."

As a priest, pastor, and teacher, it is evident that Father Hater has relied on that Spirit throughout his priestly life and ministry. I mentioned at the outset of this reflection my utter amazement at how God brings people into our lives for a given purpose. What is just as amazing to my mind is how people continue to change and adapt even as they grow older. They do not become fixed in time.

The Church that Father Hater was ordained to serve is not necessarily the same Church today. Even more so, the world is much more different and complex. Nevertheless, Father Hater continues to grow according to God's plan and adapt as needed, following the promptings of the Holy Spirit. For me, that is one of the overriding messages for anyone who reads this book. We need to be people of the Holy Spirit who practice adaptability and flexibility as needed, always in the context of the Church. We must never tire of change or lose sight of finding new ways for doing things. Above all, we cannot afford to forget that we are all members of a domestic church.

The Most Rev. David J. Bonnar
Bishop of Youngstown

Introduction

The Catholic parish is at a crossroads, brought about by a plethora of factors, including the loss of church membership, the priest scandals, the declining numbers of priests, the aging population of priests, financial difficulties, the closing and merging of parishes, and the need to help parishes devise new ways to address contemporary parish issues.

Dioceses across the country face a crisis. It centers on how to develop effective pastoral approaches with a limited number of priests. Often, there are not enough priests to carry out the ministerial responsibilities of providing adequate sacramental services. A consensus grows in dioceses that parishes need to refocus in order to address the priest shortage, but no magic formula exists to solve the problem. So, diocesan and parish leaders wonder and worry about what can be done.

At this crossroads, pastors, parish priests, and pastoral ministers face new challenges. This book does not speak to the administrative or organizational challenges faced by parishes. Rather, it concentrates on the importance of the pastor and parish leaders in assisting the faith formation of families. Furthermore, it aims to help parish leaders develop an orientation that supports families and assists parents as they raise their children in the Catholic Faith, teach them to pray, speak about Catholic matters at home with them, and introduce them to the Mass and the sacraments.

Since parents are their children's first and most important teachers of the Faith, *Evangelizing Today's Domestic Churches* addresses current challenges to family faith and offers suggestions for pastoral leaders to help them enhance parental faith, so that parents may then instill their own Faith into their children. This is no easy task, for families are challenged by secularism, atheism, and internal problems within the Church.

This book encourages pastoral leaders to help parents see the parish and family as reciprocal agents of the new evangelization, each needing the other. It aims at helping them acknowledge that the primary thrust of forming missionary disciples rests in the family, with the parish community reinforcing and supporting what happens within the domestic church — that is, what happens at home. It invites Church leaders to take another look at the domestic church, rooted in God's love.

The church of the home and the parish are both necessary, but faith formation, including catechesis, takes a different focus in each. Future parish vibrancy will depend largely on how a parish supports family life and vice versa. At the center of this endeavor are the pastor and parish priests who take the lead in helping families recognize their responsibility before God to become domestic churches.

My approach does not require parishes to develop new initiatives and programs. This book is not a *how-to*. Rather, through stories, pastoral insights, and theological reflections, it considers in a new way what is already happening in the parish and uses existing structures and programs to develop a family perspective. To accomplish this new way of seeing, the work offers an implicit threefold dynamic, found in the personal stories, biblical references, and Church documents interspersed throughout the book. This dynamic indicates the significance of stories related to the family and their influence on faith formation. The first dynamic flows from my own life story and experience as a priest for over sixty years. The second encourages pastors, parish priests, and other readers to consider their own past and present experiences and how they benefit their own ministries. A parish leader's stories are often fruitful ground for bringing to life the workings of the Holy Spirit. Jesus himself told stories, and he continues to minister in this way as he lives through our own stories. The third dynamic occurs when, after reading my stories and reflecting on one's own experiences, a parish leader relates them to the events and stories of those served through preaching and other pastoral matters. This can be done on one's own and by reflecting on the questions at the end of the chapters.

This book is divided into two parts, interspersed with questions for reflection. A brief synopsis of the layout will help orient the reader, and it will also assist priests who might use parts of the book in creating topics for their sermons.

Part one, titled "Setting the Foundation," consists of four chapters and considers the family in contemporary culture. The family is a key aspect of the People of God and takes its rightful place as a domestic church in light of it. To situate the domestic church within the broader Church, Part one looks at Jesus' home, early house churches, the domestic church after Vatican II, and the impact of culture and climate on faith formation.

Chapter one begins with present and past families and addresses challenges from contemporary culture, including COVID-19. It introduces family faith formation and briefly considers the domestic church and the digital revolution.

Chapter two considers today's families in light of the distant past. It offers lessons that families can learn from the Holy Family of Jesus, Mary, and Joseph and from Christian house churches before AD 300.

Chapter three reflects on new directions in family ministry, beginning with Vatican II. It addresses key issues arising from *Lumen Gentium*, the call to missionary discipleship, and new ecclesiological perspectives contained in recent Church documents.

Chapter four considers the significance of Catholic culture and climate in faith formation.

Part two, titled "Forming Domestic Churches," expands on the pastoral and practical issues addressed in part one. It provides insights for today's families in light of early house churches. These six chapters offer church ministers ways of being present to parishioners, guiding pastoral matters, and refocusing the parish on the family. This section includes six elements of family faith formation, flowing from the call of every Christian to proclaim the kingdom of God.

Chapter five discusses the call to relationships and their influence on a family's role as followers of Christ. It begins with early Christian disciples, considers how their mutual relationships were the basis of their house churches, and provides a fresh perspective for domestic churches.

Chapter six considers the call to accountability, hospitality, and evangelization. It reflects on what would happen if parents taught their children that a key aspect of their lives involves living out and professing that Jesus is Lord. We are all accountable for sharing this message and carrying it to the world, as Jesus' disciples did at the beginning of the Church. This requires hospitality and an evangelizing spirit.

Chapter seven reflects on the call to missionary discipleship as the Christian's response to the call to evangelize. Every Christian is called to a special role in life, each different, some more unique than others. For missionary disciples this means to follow Jesus' injunction to teach all nations.

Chapter eight studies the call to the kingdom of justice and peace. The ultimate goal of Christian family living is directed toward the kingdom of God. This area of missionary discipleship begins in the home. This chapter asks, "What does Jesus teach us about the kingdom of God and its relationship to justice and peace?"

Chapter nine looks at the call to prayer and worship. It centers on the passage from the Acts of the Apostles (Acts 2:42) that mentions four aspects of Christian living; namely, teaching, fellowship, the breaking of bread, and prayer.

Chapter ten concludes with the call to faith formation. It develops the notion that effective faith formation centers on the climate of the home. This establishes the foundation for the entire faith formation process.

The conclusion offers words of hope to Christian families striving to follow Jesus in our challenging world.

PART ONE
SETTING THE FOUNDATION

The couple that loves and begets life is a true,
living icon — not an idol like those of stone or
gold prohibited by the Decalogue — capable
of revealing God the Creator and Savior.

Pope Francis, Amoris Laetitia[1]

To set the foundation for consideration of the domestic church, Part One clarifies the term *domestic church*, shows how it relates to other dimensions of the Church, and speaks of the important role of parents in the home.

The ecclesial use of the expression *domestic church* was initiated at Vatican II. Its use harkens back to what Saint Paul referred to as the "church of the home" or a "house church."[2] The theology of the domestic church is still developing, and it is not our intention to delve into the different nuances or meanings of this expression. It's sufficient to say that variations in its meaning flow from whether one considers the domestic church as stemming primarily from baptism or from marriage. If taken in the latter sense, the scope of the term is narrower. The former use, rooted in baptism, is more extensive and can include various configurations. The more common use of the term focuses on the family, regardless of its configuration, as the most basic Christian community.

Early house churches contained various configurations and welcomed outsiders, including slaves and neighbors. Here the focus was the assembly itself, meeting in a disciple's house.

With this said, we describe a domestic church as a Christian assembly, centered in a family and gathered in a home to pray, praise God, live virtuous lives, learn the mysteries of faith, support one another in belief and practice, and participate in the mission of Christ. For our purposes, we regard the terms *domestic church, Christian house church, Christian household,* and *Christian family* as equivalent expressions.

To appreciate the domestic church in its relationship to other dimensions of the Church, it helps to clarify other ecclesial aspects of the Church, with the family as the most basic community of faith. Before Vatican II, no one spoke of the family as a domestic church. Since then, a gradual clarification of the family's relationship to the larger Church has occurred. For this reason, we schematize the Church as consisting of five aspects; namely, the domestic, parish (local), diocesan, national, and universal. Each is related to one another.

The domestic church (family) is at the core of the Church. Here, faith is born and nourished. Family faith is incomplete, however, without a parish and the diocese to sustain it.

The parish (local church), historically, has been the beacon for individuals and families to assemble to learn, profess their faith, celebrate the sacraments, and support each other. As a community of believers, the parish plays an essential role in the faith formation of Catholics. Led by a pastor, it is a beacon of hope, necessary in good and trying times. When speaking of the relationship of the parish and the diocese, the *Directory for Catechesis* says, "Having arisen from the missionary expansion of the Church, parishes have a direct connection with the particular Church, of which they are as it were a cell."[3] The parish needs diocesan support.

The diocese (particular church) is led by a bishop who follows in the footsteps of the apostles. Referring to the diocese's universal call to mission, the *Directory for Catechesis* says, "Equipped with every means by the Holy Spirit, it is up to the particular Churches to continue the work of evangelization, contributing to the good of the universal Church."[4]

The national church (nation) of a country gives assistance to the particular churches of a region. The various cultures around the world are reflected in churches of different countries.

The universal Church consists of the entire Church, as an assembly of believers united under the pope, the Bishop of Rome. A close relationship exists between these aspects of the Church,[5] especially the relationship between domestic churches and a parish church. Parishes are to support what happens in families of faith. In this endeavor, pastors play a vital role in fostering family faith, while not neglecting the ministry to single people who are parts of some family.

Pope St. John Paul II spoke of the bond that exists between the domestic and parish churches and invited pastors and parish priests to make families a top priority. In his letter *Gratissimam Sane*, when speaking to families, the pope expressed his desire "to knock at the door of your home, eager to greet you with deep affection and to spend time with you."[6]

In using these words, the pope encouraged pastors to help families recognize that they are the first and most important pathway to God. This entails figuratively knocking at the doors of their homes by affirming them in preaching and religious instruction, supporting them at difficult times, celebrating with them at Mass and the reception of the sacraments, exercising responsible stewardship, and carrying out other parish ministries. Parishes need to develop an overall family-centered attitude. This does not mean doing more by way of new programs but by doing what parish ministers do every day with renewed vigor, hope, and enthusiasm. Pope Francis says that the parish offers the main contribution to the family's pastoral care.[7] In light of this, pastoral leaders may need to focus on the ministries to families provided by their parishes.

This is no easy task. Often, parish ministers never know how their support of families and speaking about God's presence in the home bear fruit. They do not know how their words, advice, sacramental ministry, prayers, and pastoral concern make a difference in families. As Scripture says, one person sows the seed, but God gives the increase (see 1 Cor 3:6–8).

The many changes in secular and Church culture make it crucial that Church leaders examine their parish ministries to families. Many such changes have been brought about by digital technology, the uncertain conditions of families, drug crises in the home, and growing numbers of multiethnic parishes.

When change occurs, vibrant domestic churches require healthy communication with the entire Body of Christ. The Church's health depends on the relationship between the five dimensions of Church, mentioned above. Each depends on the others, and the family is at the core. Here, the first seeds of faith are planted, and they are nourished by the other dimensions.

Healthy relationships, strengthened by dialogue, are a prerequisite for a vibrant domestic church. Such relationships carry over into the world, where family members live and work. Families receive encouragement and support from solid relationships with the parish of which they are members, as well as with the diocese, national, and universal Church. These relationships are based on a fundamental relationship with the Trinity, with the

Father as the protector, Jesus as the model of fidelity, and the Holy Spirit as the nourisher in good and difficult times.

To clarify the workings of the domestic church, Vatican II used the biblical categories of priest, prophet, and king from the Old Testament when speaking of the role that parents exercise in their homes. Early Christians referred to Jesus' role as the Messiah with these words. Today, they are applied to married couples fulfilling their vocations in the domestic church of the home.

In the Mosaic law, the priestly function centered around offering sacrifices to God to praise and honor him and to atone for sins. Through his life, death, and resurrection, Jesus fulfilled this role in a most perfect way. Christian parents carry on what Jesus did in the paschal mystery when they sacrifice for their families and those around them. Liturgically, they join with other members of Jesus' Mystical Body as they celebrate the Eucharist and the other sacraments.

The prophetic role focuses on speaking for God. As God's spokesman, Jesus revealed God through his life and teaching. As members of his Mystical Body, every baptized person is called to fulfill a prophetic role. Parents do so as they teach their children about God through their words and actions.

In the Old Testament, the king was an absolute ruler, entrusted to care for his subjects. Jesus brought this kingly function to its fullest expression by offering himself as a servant leader, thus teaching us what true leadership means. Parents carry out this kingly function by giving their families examples of servant leadership and by encouraging them to serve others. As servant leaders, parents invite their children to assist the needy. In so doing, their domestic church becomes a community of service, dedicated to helping one another and reaching out to the poor and alienated. The domestic church can be a powerful symbol of what Jesus taught, as he served others.

Questions for Reflection

❏ If someone asked you how to describe the meaning of the domestic church, how would you answer?

❏ If you were to prepare a homily or catechetical session on the domestic church, how would you describe it in pastoral terms?

❏ Why is parish support for families important for parish leaders to stress in today's secular world? What are the pastoral implications of this need?

❏ What are some practical consequences for a pastor who believes that the domestic church is at the core of the Church?

❏ Do you have to be Catholic to have a domestic church? Why or why not?

Chapter One
Made, Not Born

The family is the primary setting for socialization,
since it is where we first learn to relate to others,
to listen and share, to be patient and show
respect, to help one another and live as one.

Pope Francis, Amoris Laetitia[1]

Michelle, Jason, and their two-year-old daughter, Lucy, attend Mass each Sunday. Looking at Lucy when she smiles and cries, her parents know she is a special treasure — a precious gift from God. Near them in church are the family of Sara and Jake — mother and son. They are older and less regular in their Mass attendance. The divorce of Sara and her husband shattered this family. The spiritual needs of these two families differ greatly. When a pastor or parish priest reflects on the parish family, he realizes that people of all sorts belong. Some parents, like Michelle and Jason, are sincerely interested in their family's growth in faith, while others do little to enhance it. In addition, an unknown number of families have become comfortable watching Mass on television or online during the COVID-19 pandemic. How this influences them and their children's long-term commitment to the Faith is unclear. Will they remain Catholic in the world of tomorrow?

THE WAY IT WAS

To address the future faith of Catholics, we begin with another question: Why am I Catholic today? This question reminds me of a conversation with Pinchas Peli in 1969, a noted rabbinic scholar and visiting professor at the University of Notre Dame.

On one occasion, he invited me to dinner at his home. After enjoying a relaxing meal, we discussed Catholic evangelization. I was having difficulty clarifying its meaning for a research paper. After listening to me, he said, "This is a Christian, not a Jewish, problem. Since I was born of a Jewish mother, I am Jewish." Quoting Tertullian, an early Church theologian, he said, "Christians are made, not born."[2] These words affirmed the important role that parents play in forming their children's Catholic identity.

I often reflect on Peli's words that I was not born Catholic but was formed like a beautiful painting. My parents fashioned me with brushstrokes of love and affection during countless happy days and, for them, sleepless nights. Their deep love set the stage for me to believe in Jesus, Mary, and the Church. They helped form me into the Catholic that I am today. This began early in life, when they had me baptized, and continued as they raised me in a Catholic family.

While reflecting on this conversation with Rabbi Peli, I ask myself a series of questions: Am I a Catholic today because of my family upbringing and because almost everyone I knew as a child was Catholic? Or because the nuns taught me the *Baltimore Catechism* in grade school? Or because we lived across the street from Saint William Church? Or because we went to Mass every Sunday? Or because I attended Catholic schools? Or because of the overall Catholic climate, implied in these answers, and all that I learned within it as I grew up?

I am Catholic today because the Catholic spirit or climate, fashioned by my parents and others, was paramount. Even though all the above factors influenced my faith formation, the all-embracing climate of Catholicism, epitomized by the unarticulated good example of my parents, influenced me the most.

What did this Catholic climate include? It consisted of, for example, the weekly holy hour that my father made during perpetual adoration from 2:00 to 3:00 a.m. early each Wednesday, even though he had a hard workday ahead of him. It was his leaving our dry goods store during Holy Week to go to confession. It was my first year of school, which my mother spent with me at home, teaching me about God through her words and example, because I was too sick to be in a regular class. It was the good example of the priests and nuns and the positive regard of our family for Saint William Parish. It was the fifty or more boys and girls of my age that attended morning Mass each day before walking to high school some twenty minutes away.

These seemingly little things formed the Catholic climate of our home and neighborhood that profoundly influenced me. This Catholic climate formed my identity as a Catholic. Because Catholicism was important for my family and peers, it became important to me. This era of Catholicism is over. The Catholic climate has changed drastically, and Catholic families must adjust to the changing circumstances. As the external environment becomes increasingly secular, with little thought about religion or values, committed Catholic parents need to focus on their families.

Whereas in the past, being a Catholic was more or less a given in Catholic families, today's Catholic parents need to intentionally decide to follow the Catholic way and transmit Jesus' message to their families. They do this by connecting their family as a domestic church to the parish and broader Catholic community. In this environment, parents act in the person of Christ and join with the parish to form their homes into domestic churches. With this said, there is no guarantee that every child will react the same way to a Catholic home climate. Nonetheless, it is imperative that parents and parishes join forces to present a positive picture of the Faith to children and youth. The rest is up to how young people respond to the workings of the Holy Spirit.

Today's society and Church are different from my childhood, but the basic dynamics that shape a person's identity within a specific cultural climate remain the same. With this in mind, we reflect on current challenges to the Faith.

THE WAY IT IS

Our consideration of the family as a domestic church begins by addressing challenges to the family from contemporary culture. This approach suggests that pastors and pastoral ministers consider new directions for family faith formation.

The need to refocus became clear to me while I was teaching pastoral ministry courses in Catholic colleges for over fifty years. In recent times, many parents have asked the same question: "Why have my children left the Catholic Church? We prayed at home, were active in our parish, and went to Mass every Sunday. Our children attended Catholic schools, and we encouraged them to live by the Church's teachings."

In public and private conversations, parents have said, "As

our children grew into their teens, they missed Sunday Mass, as soccer, baseball, music lessons, and other activities took precedence. Sometimes it was our fault, for we excused their absence from Mass for what now appear to be trite reasons. In addition, some of our children disagree with Church teaching on birth control, gay and lesbian matters, and even abortion. They put more credence into what their friends say and what they learn on the internet than what we taught them."

Many parents have also said, "The priest scandal and the bishops' cover-up made matters worse. Then, when parishes shut down during the pandemic, this solidified our children's thinking that Mass attendance was not that important. They say that praying to God is enough. Although many Catholic young people remain faithful to the Church, an increasing number are leaving." No simple answers exist to address these challenging issues.

Pastors and parish priests often hear these concerns. So do deacons, catechists, and those engaged in faith formation. As parents wonder, they also ask themselves, What did we do wrong? What else should we have done that we failed to do? Can we do anything to fix it? A good response to those who tried sincerely to raise their children Catholic is: "You have done nothing wrong. Your child is responsible for his or her decisions. How they are before God can only be known by God."

Parents need to encourage their adult children to follow the practices of their faith, even if they have stopped going to Mass or do not have their own children baptized. Their sons and daughters need support and guidance as they discern what to do.

No simple answers or magic fixes exist to help adult children continue in the Faith. To address the issue of staying in or leaving the Church involves looking at how our consciences and value systems are formed by family values, the secular culture, peer pressure, and the digital world, especially social media.

The present situation makes one thing clear: For tomorrow's families, especially our youth, to remain Catholics, it cannot be business as usual in liturgical and catechetical formation. Many parish ministerial efforts are not as effective as they should be in spite of using excellent catechetical, liturgical, and digital tools.

Pastors need to look at the effectiveness of their parish ministries to children, youth, and young adults. Such effectiveness does not mean making liturgical ceremonies more appealing, developing better catechetical materials, or teaching doctrinal content down to the smallest jot and tittle. This has already been done, often to little avail. Something more radical is needed, which requires an approach to faith formation that takes a clue from the past and focuses on the family.

Effective parish ministry stands at a threshold, challenged by many questions. Will the parish become a more vibrant force for good, or will its influence wane in an increasingly secular world? Will the trend of Catholics leaving the Faith intensify or lessen? Will Catholic parishes and schools develop new ways to impact the faith of students? Will families receive needed direction from their pastors and other Church leaders?

Pastors, parish priests, and their pastoral staffs are encouraged to address such critical questions, not shove them under the rug as if they did not exist. How our youth and Catholics generally respond to the new face of the Church will depend on a variety of factors, beginning with how God comes to us.

GOD COMES TO FAMILIES

To address how God comes to us, let's consider that different experiences shape our values, attitudes, and beliefs. Growing children process their experiences consciously and unconsciously, and parents help them sort out right from wrong. God comes to us in the complex web of such experiences, illustrated by the following story:

When considering how my value system was formed, I recall an event from my childhood. When I was about seven years old, I found a rubber innertube from a bike. This was a cherished item during the Second World War, when rubber was scarce. Since the innertube was split apart, I decided to make a sling shot from it to shoot pebbles and rocks. One afternoon, I saw a tree limb shaped in a Y. It was the right size, so I cut it, split the innertube into strips, and found a piece of leather to make the sling for a rock.

When finished, I was proud of what I made. A friend and I put a tin can on the fence behind the house, and we shot at it. Once, a bird flew past us and sat on the top of the fence post. I shot at the bird, and I think I hit it. I felt terrible when I saw the bird fall.

Did the bird die? I wasn't sure, for when I looked for it, I couldn't find it. Did it fly away, or did I miss seeing it on the ground? Afterwards, I felt too guilty to tell my parents and kept it inside of myself. In retrospect, this act significantly influenced my belief about not hurting another animal or human.

It was a simple act, but one that left an indelible mark. It illustrates how hundreds of such instances, from being punched by a neighborhood kid to having an old man help me make a victory garden in an abandoned lot behind my house, affected my value system. Even more than such childhood acts that influenced my value formation, my Catholic upbringing deeply affected me. When almost every neighbor was Catholic, we were convinced that Catholics had the true Faith. We knew little about Protestants, but my experience with the kind old man, described above, who helped me in my garden, made me wonder why he, a Protestant, was so nice, helpful, and patient, and why some Catholics were just the opposite.

Unbeknown to me, the Catholic culture slowly shaped my values. Only later did I realize how it exercised more influence on me than what I learned from books. This applied especially in my home, where my parents exercised the greatest influence. As I grew, my experiences with the Catholic Church were positive, as were my Catholic grade and high school years. I loved my classmates and the nuns who taught us. We had a group of saintly pastors and priests in our parish. Mass, Communion, and hanging around the parish were ordinary occurrences as we matured. Such early experiences strengthened my faith for adult life. When our grade school class celebrated our seventieth anniversary of our graduation, we still spoke glowingly of those early years, when values were formed — some positive, others negative, but all with love.

Such influential events in early childhood accompanied me through high school, college, seminary, ordination, and the rest of my life. From them, I learned that each person is unique before God. What happens to us along life's path affects who we are and what we become. For this reason, for better or for worse, no child in a family is like any other sibling, and no adult can transfer his or her values automatically to his or her children.

God comes to young children, youth, and adults differently. Our Faith is incarnational. This means that the Lord comes to us through our experiences in nature, in relationships within the family, in the broader culture, and in the environment of our Catholic parish. Paramount among these is the family, the greatest single influence on anyone. My parents played a powerful role in how God's presence came to me.

CHALLENGES FROM THE SECULAR CULTURE AND CHURCH

God comes to us differently from person to person, situation to situation. This is not because God changes, but because family, culture, and religion filter God's presence differently.

In reflecting on our life story, we recognize that God comes to us in the culture and times in which we live. Today's social context has a different focus than when I was a child. Early in my life, my parents, neighbors, friends, and parish played prominent roles in my value formation.

Today, the internet, social media, and television expose children and youth to various influences, many of them negative. Parents no longer have the same impact on the faith formation of their children, especially when they are not committed to the Faith.

Although parents still exercise the strongest role in faith formation, digital media and peers play a big role in presenting the values that young people internalize. As the *General Directory for Catechesis* says, "Parents are the primary educators in the faith. Together with them, especially in certain cultures, all members of the family play an active part in the education of the younger members."[3]

As parents encourage their children in these challenging times, it is imperative that they teach them, by word and example, the basic truths of the Faith, especially the objective norms of right and wrong that offer us a roadmap for a healthy life. These norms are often included under the natural law. Relativism minimizes these universal norms, in effect denying them. Its pervasiveness in our culture provides a great challenge when teaching youth that definite moral values and ways of acting exist, instead of making them subjective for every person.

In our imperfect world, good and evil forces struggle to influence our beliefs and how we act. What is clear and certain for one person may be cloudy for another. How we interpret reality often depends on the beliefs and attitudes learned in a family or a social group. In this regard, what a parent believes may differ from what a child accepts as true.

Although objective norms of conduct exist, not everyone accepts them. We need to encourage our children to form their consciences according to correct norms of behavior, for the conscience, formed appropriately, is our ultimate norm of morality. A family, living as a domestic church, accepts moral values consistent with Jesus' message and the Church's teachings.

As parents teach their children what is right, they also recognize that every generation faces new obstacles. This is challenging for Catholic families, who see increasing pressures from inside and outside the Church.

Challenges from outside the Church can be summarized by examining four chief characteristics that our culture presents to families. The United States Army War College developed a schema in the 1990s and referred to it as a "VUCA world"; it highlights the Volatility, Uncertainty, Complexity, and Ambiguity of our times. These characteristics of the modern world offer challenges for pastors, pastoral leaders, and parents when dealing with matters pertaining to the domestic church. The culture that parishes and families face is volatile and unstable. It changes at a rapid pace and in unpredictable ways. Parents deal with issues such as: What will the future hold for our children? How can we deal with our pent-up feelings?

The uncertainty in our culture makes it difficult to predict what will happen next, as new issues surface for parishes and families. These include: Should a child go to college and be strapped with a huge debt or pursue another future such as the military or a skilled trade? How will digital learning affect our future parish catechesis and family relationships? To address such questions, new paradigms are required, for previous ways of doing things may not work.

Our complex culture has many interconnected parts that are confusing and cause uncertainty. The constant bombardment with data makes it difficult to process which information is helpful (and even correct) and how to respond to it all. Families and Church communities find themselves deluged regarding what to do, with little advice on how to do it.

Our ambiguous culture offers us little precedent regarding the present situation, where much anger, frustration, and a lack of clarity exist about what certain events mean. Parents and parishes often are uncertain about the future for their children and look for direction in a directionless society. As Archbishop José Gomez says, "Our society has rejected what twenty centuries of Christian civilization considered a basic fact of nature — that most men and women will find their life's purpose in forming loving marriages, working together, sharing their lives, and raising children."[4]

Let's keep his words in mind as we face challenges from outside the Church that take their toll as the Church deals with them and the direction our broader culture has taken, especially during and after the pandemic. To what degree the pandemic will enhance the secularization of society — or diminish it by causing the secular culture to get down on its spiritual knees — is yet to be determined. As far as faith formation is concerned, it has already influenced Mass attendance, Church meetings, business affairs, and developing materials for faith formation.

Catholic families experience challenges from within the Church, which influence the faith community. These include those arising from the priest shortage, the declining number of Catholics at Mass, and the effects of the clerical scandal. The latter led to a negative image of the Church, the distrust of the clergy, and people leaving the Faith.

What does this say to those living the Catholic way of life? Among other things, it challenges them to a deeper appreciation of being Catholic, as this has been handed down from the apostles through Sacred Tradition.

Pastors also face pressures arising from the priest shortage, since not enough priests are in the United States to adequately meet the sacramental needs of parishioners. Many aging pastors wonder how much longer they can go on. Looking at the demographics and age of the clergy indicates that something must be done.

No magic formula exists to answer the internal challenges that parishes face. Pastors need to rely on the wisdom given by the Holy Spirit, focus on the needs of the Catholic community, and stress the importance of the parish in its relationship with the domestic church.

As one effort to revitalize the parish, the Congregation of the Clergy published an instruction[5] on the parish in July 2020. It stressed the parish's missionary role and focused on the changing nature of parishes. It noted that some existing parishes will become megachurches with large congregations, others will decline in membership, and still others will merge, close, or develop new configurations to better serve the People of God.

As this process of changing parish configuration is occurring slowly, it's too early to anticipate the future structure and style of parish ministries. What becomes clear, however, is that whatever configuration future parishes take, parents increasingly will be challenged to form their own families in the Faith. This will be necessary as the number of professional catechetical leaders declines and fewer parishes compensate for this loss by developing first-class ways to configure catechesis for children and youth.

With hybrid ways to educate children in the Faith emerging from digital media, parishes can employ the best ways available to help families move forward spiritually. As with secular subjects, digital platforms are now used by Catholic publishers to fill a catechetical void and to come up with new ways to share the Faith. While parishes and families strive to support each other, these companies are setting the catechetical tone for the future. In many instances, the focus of their catechetical materials is shifting from the target audience of teachers and parish leaders to families, especially parents.

Today, the challenge of secular culture is strong, as committed Catholic parents look for ways to catechize their families. While advances have been made in using technology for faith formation, many parents are uncertain about how to proceed into the future. They search for answers and a Faith community to support them.

This gives pastors the opportunity to touch something deep and fundamental in parishioners through their words, compassion, and especially the sacramental life of the Church. In this regard, relationships are paramount. Pope Francis stresses that for the word of God to be effectively communicated, encounter is essential. This means that homilies should be presented with a flavor that inspires those present to see that the Christian Faith gives them answers for what is missing in the secular world.

CHANGING FAMILY FAITH FORMATION

In the first years of my priesthood, as I gave instruction to prepare couples for marriage, I used notes from my seminary class on marriage. They described in a straightforward way the nature of marriage. In retrospect, my approach covered over the fact that I knew little about the real issues facing married couples.

When I began giving these marriage instructions, prior to Vatican II, the secular and religious roles of parents and children were clearly set by culture. Men worked, and most women cared for the home. Few girls from my elementary school class went to college. Most married and began their families in their early twenties. Families usually had only one automobile. As far as religion was concerned, it was unthinkable to miss Mass on Sunday, a day dedicated to the Lord. Parishioners respected the priests and nuns. I was born into a stable society, and the emotional stress was not as pronounced as it is today.

During the hectic 1960s, the secular and Catholic mentalities shifted focus, and so did families. In this new environment, Catholics struggled to adjust. Masses changed from Latin to English, and ways of instructing children in the Faith also changed. Women increasingly worked outside the home, and daycare centers for children became necessary. Church teachings on birth control were rejected by some Catholics. Many stopped going to confession. What was happening in the broader society impacted faith formation. No longer were things cut-and-dried in the Catholic community.

As Catholic families changed, children's sports, dance lessons, and other activities often replaced attendance at Sunday Mass. As family life shifted, priests and sacramental ministers struggled to find effective ways to prepare Catholic couples for marriage and family life.

Changes in the attitudes and practices of Catholics solidified during the final quarter of the last century and into the beginning of the third millennium. Today, the increasing demands of a technological world bring tensions that press in on families, making it difficult for parents to fulfill their responsibilities.

Over the years, I have changed my approach in assisting engaged couples. Initially, I taught engaged couples the Church's basic teachings regarding marriage but did little to include practical ways to help them set a solid course for their future family. Now I see that preparation for a married couple's family life begins in the attitudes and values developed in their families of origin. This plays a big role when they begin their own family.

In our secular culture, there is no easy way to effectively address engaged couples. It is important, however, for Church ministers to encourage engaged couples to make a commitment to live as a Catholic family when a man and woman begin marriage instruction. This must be stressed during the course of marriage preparation and repeated at baptismal preparation after children are born.

Society continues to change, and so does the Church. Being born into a Catholic family no longer guarantees that children will be raised Catholic or remain faithful to the Church. Being Catholic, in addition, no longer means that a family will be faithful to Sunday Mass attendance and committed to live the Catholic way.

As massive changes occur in the broader society, Catholic parishes must respond accordingly. Two suggestions are offered for parish family ministry. These are: (1) For the parish, focus ministries on the family, and reinforce what is happening within them; (2) for families, encourage parents to make a deliberate and intentional choice to live their Catholic Faith. The first suggestion is discussed more at length when addressing the family as a domestic church. Here, we concentrate on the second suggestion, which focuses on intentionality.

Put simply, *intentionality* in this context means that sometime before or after marriage, a married couple makes a definite decision to be a Catholic family, with all this implies, and to take necessary steps to make it happen. The pastor and parish leaders can recommend this for all Catholic families and affirm its importance in liturgical and other ministries. This is necessary because of how our attitudes and values are formed. Let's briefly consider why this is so.

In a relatively closed society, like the Catholic Church before Vatican II, preconscious dynamics set the tone for the attitudes and actions of individual Catholics, families, parishes, and the universal Church. These dynamics influenced what Catholics believed and how they acted. For example, it was understood that Catholics never ate meat on Friday or missed Mass on Sunday. They believed that to knowingly and willingly do so was a mortal sin. Catholics never questioned these beliefs; they just practiced them. Powerful dynamics, coming from the collective preconscious awareness of Catholics, influenced their way of living and told them that this was how it had to be.

The same applied to much of what Catholics did. This included strong suggestions for Catholic men and women that they date only Catholics. It also meant following the norms dictating how Catholics lived their moral lives, why they respected nuns and priests, and more. Powerful dynamics implicitly set the tone for how personal and family life was lived. Priests reinforced this "Catholic way" in their teaching and sermons. Catholic catechisms and religion books taught it. This undergirded what children learned from their parents and from their teachers. It told children and adults what was right, what was wrong, and how Catholics should live and act.

Vatican II shattered this collective awareness of the Catholic way. When Catholics were questioning, religious freedom and conscience formation were encouraged by the Church, while other aspects of the Faith, once accepted without questions — such as the morality of artificial birth control — were brought to consciousness. Then, Catholics said yes to some of them and no to others. This set the stage for how Catholics respond today, and it changed how best to instruct Catholics in the Faith.

SHIFTING TO THE DOMESTIC CHURCHES

When I was a child, our family's Catholic Faith centered around the parish. When anyone asked me where I was from, my answer was: "I'm from Saint William's Parish." In high school, when I asked my classmates the same question, their answers were: "I'm from Saint Theresa Parish," or "Resurrection Parish," or "Saint Dominic Parish." Our identities as people and as Catholics were very much tied to our parishes.

We grew up this way, and the parish, including the pastor, became a key aspect of our lives. Often appointed as pastor of a parish for life, he was symbolic of the Church. We applauded his strengths and tolerated his weaknesses. In a sense, he was part of our families. In our parish, we always knew when "Father R." was driving down our streets, because he never took his stick-shift Buick out of second gear. We celebrated and suffered with him, and he with us. He was at home walking up and down the streets, greeting parishioners, stopping to sit on their front porches, and laughing with the children, illustrated by the following episode:

I recall the time when the fire department danger signals rang out in the neighborhood, and the ladder wagon rumbled toward Saint William Church. Smoke poured from the church, and we soon learned that someone had tried to set it on fire. After the fire was controlled, our old pastor walked slowly up the street and sat on our front steps with our family. With tears in his eyes he said, "Why would anyone want to do this?"

His love of the parishioners and their love for him speak eloquently of this era. For us, the pastor represented the Church, and Catholic families were part of this wonderful community.

Times have changed, but our excursion into the past typifies how things were in the mid-twentieth century. Although deeply committed to the Faith, Catholics never thought of individual families as domestic churches, as we do today.

Coupled with an awareness of the family as a domestic church, we need new stories of how today's families can be described in this way. We also need new models to reflect how today's parish is a significant aspect of family life. These models have to develop vibrant connections between the parish, diocese, universal Church, and the domestic church of the home.

The *Catechism* of *the Catholic Church* speaks of the family as the domestic church, but it doesn't develop this idea. The Catholic community is beginning to appreciate, however, the implications of regarding families as domestic churches. The next step is to help Catholic families better understand what this means for them.

For this to happen, families need support from their pastors and pastoral staffs, as well as a commitment to gospel values to guide them. Keeping this in mind, parents can ask: Who are the role models from our Faith Tradition, and how do their relationships with the culture where they lived help us deal with the uncertainty that we now experience?

In order to identify these role models, chapter two looks at how Christianity began with the coming of Jesus, and then it moves in two directions. First, it looks to the Holy Family as a model for today's family. The times when they lived were different from today, but the personal dynamics they experienced were similar to those we face. Second, it looks at early house churches as providing a model for modern families. (Further on, part two of this book proposes seven key elements in these house churches that are applicable today.)

Questions for Reflection

❑ How often do you connect the readings at Mass to your life experiences or current issues facing families in the parish?

❑ In what ways can technology and digital media help pastors and parish leaders more effectively communicate the word of God in homilies and catechetical sessions?

❑ From your experience, what are significant topics that people need to hear in homilies?

❑ What events in your life had a significant impact on your faith and ministry?

❑ How do the challenges of a VUCA world influence your ministry?

❑ How is the Holy Family a model for today's families?

❑ How can pastors and pastoral ministers help their congregations make deliberate choices to live their lives as active Catholics?

❑ What are key elements in the shifts occurring in today's society that influence your ministry?

❑ How can a focus on families as domestic churches influence the ministry of pastoral leaders and the parish?

❑ What are significant ways that parishes can support today's domestic churches?

Chapter Two
Today's Families in Light of the Past

Every family should look to the icon of the
Holy Family of Nazareth. Its daily life had its
share of burdens and even nightmares.

Pope Francis, Amoris Laetitia[1]

Many families, struggling with job loss, the sickness of a child, or old age, sit in our congregations each week. They come to Mass for support and to hear comforting words, as they search for answers. Parents look to pastors and parish priests for a word of comfort, and they search for role models to guide them.

They usually begin with their families of origin, remembering holy ancestors that influenced them on their faith journey. In addition, they look for wisdom from their religious Tradition.

This chapter addresses the wisdom gleaned from the Holy Family, which was reflected in early house churches.

LEARNING FROM THE HOLY FAMILY[2]

When ministering to families, pastors and pastoral staffs can learn from the Holy Family. In reflecting on the lives of Jesus, Mary, and Joseph, they discover love and affection but also pain, strife and disappointments, not unlike what families experience today.

To get a clearer picture of how the Holy Family can comfort families, let's begin with what our parents, Church ministers, Scripture, and Sacred Tradition have taught us about Jesus' family. When I was a child, I considered the Holy Family as a perfect family. Their lives inspired Christian families, but it was not easy relating the Holy Family to the families that I knew. They were not perfect — a far cry from the Holy Family. It was hard to see how these families compared to the Holy Family.

As I've grown older, I've asked: How perfect was the Holy Family? Is *perfect* the right word to use, or might it be better to say that the Holy Family was a healthy yet struggling family, like every family? By *healthy*, I mean a family that deals with its struggles, traumas, disappointments, and brokenness in a healthy way.

In discussing the domestic church, current challenges to families invite pastors and pastoral staffs to reflect on families in light of the Holy Family. In so doing, they may wonder: How does the Holy Family connect with today's families?

We begin by asking: Is there a way to look at the Holy Family as a healthy yet struggling family that is faithful to Christian Tradition and speaks to contemporary families? To address this question, we consider the infancy narratives, developed in the

Gospels of Matthew and Luke. Here, there are paths of understanding that will speak to modern families, for the biblical narratives shed light on the question: Was the Holy Family a perfect family, or was it a struggling yet healthy family?

Matthew's Gospel describes Joseph, Mary's husband, as a righteous man (see Mt 1:19) who listened to God and made difficult decisions based on his Hebrew beliefs. Mary's faith inspired her to say yes to whatever God had in store for her (Lk 1:26–38). She was blessed by God and called herself the Lord's handmaid (Lk 1:48). Jesus was an obedient child with a strong self-image (Lk 2:41–52). These descriptions of Joseph, Mary, and Jesus have nourished generations of closely-knit families and continue to guide family relationships.

Matthew and Luke reveal that the Holy Family was a healthy, well-adjusted family — but a struggling one. They experienced difficulties like everyone else. The scriptural accounts of the Holy Family indicate that they suffered pain and uncertainty during Jesus' conception, birth, and early adolescence. This combination of happiness and struggle is consistent with Jesus' message of love.

Today's families need to hear the comforting words that God cares for each person, but the road to salvation involves pain and suffering. Like the Holy Family, families in our time need to rely on God's love to weather stormy moments.

By exploring the broken aspects of Jesus' family, today's families, regardless of their configurations, can better appreciate God's love for them and God's desire to heal family wounds. The infancy narratives are a good starting point to ponder the joys and sufferings of the Holy Family. Let's turn now to these narratives and focus on the broken aspects of the Holy Family's life.

Jesus' Genealogy and Conception

Matthew and Luke describe Jesus' early life and look at the

events surrounding it in the infancy narratives. These biblical stories were not intended to provide exact historical information concerning Jesus' birth and childhood. The authors were more interested in capturing the meaning of an event rather than in reporting precise details of its occurrence. Matthew and Luke provide varying accounts of the birth of Jesus (see Matthew 1:1—2:23 and Luke 2:1–52).

The infancy narratives are faith-statements reflecting the Christian belief in God's love for humankind. Both accounts give us glimpses into the pain and hurt at the heart of the Holy Family, while God's love for them is strong. Seen from this perspective, the accounts offer Christians the model of a healthy family struggling through brokenness to discover freedom and peace.

When examining the biblical references to the Holy Family, it becomes clear that "the mystery of the Word of God's becoming incarnate within a family reveals how it is the privileged place for God's revelation to humanity. ... Christian people look to the Holy Family of Nazareth as a model in relationships and love, as a point of reference for every family and as a comfort in time of trial."[3]

People today are often fascinated when discovering their family roots. This knowledge gives them a sense of belonging to something greater than themselves. The accounts of Jesus' genealogy in Matthew and Luke trace Jesus' lineage through Joseph, a common practice in patriarchal cultures. The infancy narratives provide an interesting and revealing look at Jesus' ancestors.

Matthew traces Jesus' line back through David to Abraham. In doing so, he reminds the Christian community that Jesus' birth fulfills the Messianic promises made to Abraham and to the royal house of David. Hence, there is a strong connection to Jesus' Jewish roots. Luke describes Jesus as the Son of God and shows that salvation in Jesus is extended to all humankind. He traces Jesus' roots back to Adam, the father of humankind.

In ancient times, genealogies often stressed a person's renowned ancestors. Matthew and Luke do this in constructing Jesus' genealogy. Despite differences, both evangelists indicate that Jesus was of Davidic descent, sprang from Joseph's line, and was conceived by the power of the Holy Spirit.

At the same time, some men and women in Jesus' genealogy were sinners or foreigners. Their inclusion implies a broken condition in Jesus' ancestry and hints at the mystery of God's power to overcome any obstacle in preparing the world for the Savior. By including a wide variety of people with saintly and questionable backgrounds alike, Matthew sets the tone for the rest of his Gospel.

The genealogies in Matthew and Luke indicate that Jesus assumed a broken human condition from the beginning of his life. By introducing their Gospels with Jesus' genealogy, Matthew and Luke establish a pattern which permeates all four Gospels — namely, that God is present in all human circumstances, works through different kinds of people, and heals broken lives.

The tension between happy yet broken family relationships surfaced when, before their marriage, Joseph heard about Mary's pregnancy (see Mt 1:18–20). Matthew and Luke proclaim that this pregnancy was of the Holy Spirit and was not therefore the result of an ordinary conception (Lk 1:26–38). The reader might ask: Why was Jesus conceived during Mary's betrothal to Joseph and before the wedding feast? The timing of Mary's pregnancy before marriage and the method of conception through the Holy Spirit's power might seem to be a curious way of announcing Jesus' coming into the world.

Jesus was conceived under unusual circumstances. We can hypothesize that gossip surrounded the Holy Family when people learned of Jesus' conception. Nonetheless, by trusting God, Mary and Joseph survived the pain inflicted by those who misjudged their situation. In these Gospel narratives, struggling families can find courage and hope, realizing that God's love can heal family wounds.

Luke pictures Mary as unmarried and pregnant. He describes her as confident that the child is of God. Regardless of her faith, Mary's struggle must have been tremendous. Alone and pregnant, she faced Joseph, her family, and friends with only the assurance that God was with her. She had no guarantees that anyone would understand her condition.

The story of Mary, a young woman pregnant before marriage, sends a resounding message to all women who are in like circumstances. They, like Mary, may feel alone and lost, their reputations ruined. Sometimes the father of the child, a friend, or parent may pressure her to get an abortion. When this happens, the woman can gain great strength from Mary. Although her child was of the Holy Spirit, the pain and embarrassment she suffered can give today's women who find themselves pregnant outside of wedlock the courage to carry the child and give that child the love he or she deserves. In homilies and catechesis, this connection can be a powerful incentive to keep an unplanned child, conceived in or out of wedlock.

The need for trust in God is brought home in the following story.

A young teenage girl, about Mary's age, became pregnant. The pastor of her parish spoke to her and her family on numerous occasions, stressing the beauty of life and birth and the need to have faith in God. As the family worked through the girl's pregnancy, they concluded, "We don't know what the future will hold; neither did Mary, Jesus' mother. We do know, however, that if we have faith and courage, God will be with this child. What the baby will become, we do not know, but with support from our family and God, we will be blessed, and so will the child to be born."

The faith of this family reflects Mary's faith in her response to the angel at the Annunciation (see Lk 1:26–38) and during her subsequent visit to Elizabeth (Lk 1:39–56). The Visitation account implies the Christian belief in the absolute need for faith, especially in difficult times. Here, Mary describes herself as the servant of the Lord. Through faith, God transforms Mary's fear, loneliness, and pain into hope, peace, and fruitfulness.

Mary's struggle as an unwed, pregnant teenager is also reflected in the response of Joseph, to whom she was betrothed. Matthew's Gospel concentrates on Joseph's dilemma after he discovers Mary is pregnant (see Mt 1:18–25). While he struggles to do the right thing, God enlightens him in a dream. Joseph trusts God and stands by his fiancé. Matthew describes him as a faithful listener to God, who trusts in an unknown and uncertain future. His story is a beautiful reminder of the importance of supporting those we love in difficult times.

Mary's and Joseph's struggles during Jesus' conception is the story of their life and all human life. It speaks to the society in which we now live. Their faith grew over time as they listened to God. Their yes became stronger because they believed in God's abiding presence.

Jesus' Birth and Early Life

Jesus' birth marks a turning point in history, for it shows humans as the special focus of God's love. Jesus was born away from his home, into an imperfect world, in impoverished circumstances. Luke describes shepherds visiting the young family (see Lk 2:15–19). In Jesus' time, many shepherds were poor and destitute. They often stole in order to survive and were not considered entirely trustworthy. By including shepherds at Jesus' birth, Luke depicts the poor and sinners as among the first to recognize the Savior of the world.

Matthew, on the other hand, has wealthy astrologers traveling from distant places to pay the child homage (see Mt 2:1–12).

They look for a king and find one in the lowliest place. As Gentiles, the Magi are not part of the child's Jewish family. Matthew's story underlines the royal nature of Jesus' birth and emphasizes the role of nonfamily members in recognizing the importance of his birth. After the Magi's visit, the family flees to Egypt before returning home to Nazareth. While the family remains in exile, soldiers massacre innocent children.

The circumstances surrounding Jesus' birth into an imperfect world contain implications for contemporary families. God is present to all kinds of families — abandoned spouses and children, families who leave their countries because of political or economic turmoil, the poor, the wealthy, nonChristians and Christians alike, people living in poverty, girls getting pregnant out of wedlock, unwed mothers and fathers, or those suffering the anguish of separation and divorce.

Much anguish and uncertainty about the future existed in Jesus' family. During these troubled times, Jesus' parents showed an abiding trust in God's providence. The Magnificat (Lk 1:46–55) complements the words Simeon spoke to Mary after Jesus' birth: "And a sword will pierce your own soul too" (Lk 2:35).

Luke depicts Mary as a struggling, faithful person in her ambiguous situation. Mary's response to God's actions in her life symbolizes the need to be open to God, even in difficult situations. To respond as Mary did, a person must believe that God is always present, even when the future outcome is not clear.

Families can take consolation from Jesus' family who, like theirs, was a struggling family. The cultural times were very different, but the dynamics of struggling to remain healthy and whole are similar. Like them, it is a challenge for us to remain healthy in the midst of ambiguity.

EARLY HOUSE CHURCHES AND BEYOND

Contemporary Catholic families face challenges from within

and without, as did early Christian house churches. The latter endured persecution and rejection from society. Today's domestic churches face the external challenges of materialism, individualism, secularism, digital media, and society in general. Additionally, both early house churches and our domestic churches face challenges from within the Church itself.

Pastors and pastoral staffs can learn from the early Church the importance of the domestic church and devise ways to get this message across to parishioners. This happens not by developing new ministries or establishing new organizational structures but by refocusing existing parish ministries in light of the family.

House Churches: What Were They?[4]

After Pentecost, the disciples faced the challenge of proclaiming Jesus and his message to a troubled world. The first Christians were Jewish. It was natural that what they learned in their families and in the synagogue influenced them.

We learn of house churches from the writings of Saint Paul, the Acts of the Apostles, and elsewhere. The first Christians gathered in homes for fellowship, support, prayer, and celebrating the Eucharist. These assemblies included a variety of people — family members, relatives, those living in close proximity, and slaves.

They were a family in a broad sense; their unity rested in their mutual faith in Jesus' resurrection and their commitment to share in his work as early missionary disciples. When persecution arose, many Christians found support in these house churches.

The expression *house church* is alluded to in the letters of Saint Paul. In Romans we read: "Greet Prisca and Aquila … Greet also the church in their house" (Rom 16:3–5). Also, Saint Paul says, "To Philemon our dear friend and co-worker, to Apphia our sister … and to the church in your house" (Phlm 1:1–2).

The family-based religious formation in these households had its roots in Jewish tradition.

Today, in viewing the family as a domestic church, we gain insights as we consider core elements of these early house churches. The Acts of the Apostles offers a glimpse into what happened in these Christian households. It says, "Day by day, as they spent much time together in the temple, they broke bread at home and ate their food with glad and generous hearts, praising God and having the goodwill of all the people" (Acts 2:46–47).

What dynamics existed in these early households that formed the disciples into committed missionary disciples? What essential elements were present in these Christian gatherings? Above all, the driving force of early Christian house churches was their deep conviction that Jesus, the crucified Son of God, was raised up by the Father to proclaim salvation for all people. This motivated them to act in Jesus' name, for the Acts of the Apostles says, "With great power the apostles gave their testimony to the resurrection of the Lord Jesus" (Acts 4:33).

Basic Elements of House Churches

How did these house churches make such a difference in an alien society? To address this question, let us summarize the basic elements of these Christian communities. These reflections serve as a prelude to developing them further in part two of this book, which speaks of ministry to today's families in light of the early house churches. In all of this, a pastor's role in stressing the call to missionary discipleship, shared by all the baptized, becomes clearer.

House churches recognized the elements below as vital aspects of the Christian call to follow Jesus. As a model for today, they include the following.

Relationships. In the Acts of the Apostles, we recognize the central role of care and concern exhibited by the first Christian communities. Tertullian, in the second century, wrote, "See how they love one another" (*Apology*, Chapter 39). Love motivated many pagans to join the Church.

Acknowledging the centrality of love in leading a happy life, Pope Francis stresses the vital role that encounter and dialogue play in families. He writes, "Dialogue is essential for experiencing, expressing and fostering love in marriage and family life."[5] The pope's sentiments take their roots from the first Christian households, where the disciples of Christ witnessed and learned what Jesus meant when he said, "I give you a new commandment, that you love one another. Just as I have loved you, you also should love one another" (Jn 13:34). For the disciples, relationships were important, as they gathered to support one another, pray, learn about their newfound Faith, and celebrate the Eucharist.

Accountability, Hospitality, and Evangelization. Smaller Christian communities that met in private homes were more conducive to developing hospitality and accountability. Everyone knew everyone else and expected them to be faithful to the message of Christ and the teachings of the apostles. Congregational consensus enhanced agreement on clear lines of responsibility. These house church members learned about and then proclaimed Jesus' message to others, while they supported one another.

Kindness, love, and commitment, present in early Christian gatherings, attracted neighbors and civic officials. Hence, the Church grew. Families today can learn an important lesson from these house churches, as they relate to one another and to the larger society.

Missionary Discipleship. The first Christians believed that Jesus called them to be missionary disciples. To justify this belief, they looked to Jesus' great commission, recorded in Matthew 28:19, in which he told his followers to "go therefore and make disciples of all nations." Jesus sent them on a mission to proclaim his message to the world. Their missionary endeavors began in their homes. In their house churches, early Christians took Jesus' command seriously. When he told them to teach all nations, they understood that these words were spoken to all the baptized. They carried out Jesus' command, for as Acts 5:42 says, "[E]very day in the temple and at home they did not cease to teach and proclaim Jesus as the Messiah."

The conviction of being called to be missionary disciples received energy and focus in these Christian households. This is manifest especially in the house churches described by Saint Paul, which played a prominent role in missionary activity. These Christian assemblies functioned as cells in larger towns and were the foundation for missionary work.

Prayer and Worship. "They [the disciples] devoted themselves to the apostles' teaching and fellowship, to the breaking of bread and the prayers" (Acts 2:42). Although early Christians met in the temple, home was the natural place to foster intimacy, pray, and break bread. As the Acts of the Apostles says, "Day by day, as they spent much time together in the temple, they broke bread at home and ate their food with glad and generous hearts" (Acts 2:46).

Breaking bread symbolizes sharing what one has with others. It reaches its zenith in Jesus' offering himself in the Eucharist. Contemporary families are blessed when they recognize that sharing love, sacrifice, and devotion as a family is a valuable prelude to appreciate Jesus' offering of himself for us in the Eucharist.

Prayer was central to early Christian communities. Jesus was their model for prayer as they met together, fostered fellowship, taught, endured suffering, and underwent martyrdom. Like Jesus, the apostles dedicated themselves to prayer, illustrated in their careful selection of deacons to minister to the poor, so they could spend more time in prayer and the ministry of the Word. Peter's sermon on Pentecost stressed prayer as an important way of following Christ. The community of disciples prayed as they awaited the second coming of Christ.

Prayer is the energy that often keeps families going in troubled times. Developing a relationship with God through family prayer is a beautiful way to imitate Jesus' life, as he prayed to "[l]et the little children come to me" (Mt 19:14). As he did for them, so will he do for our families, if we stay close to him in prayer.

Justice for the Poor. Like Jesus, early Christian communities focused on ministering to the poor. In Galatians, when Paul returned to Jerusalem after being gone for years, he said that the Church leaders — James, Cephas, and John — supported his ministry to the Gentiles, while asking "that we remember the poor, which was actually what I was eager to do" (Gal 2:3–10).

The commitment to justice and peace, begun in the first house churches, became the model for all subsequent Christian endeavors. It is especially important today. In remembering this obligation to reach out to the poor, we can see more clearly the connection between them and Jesus, present in their midst. I witnessed this connection in a man I met years ago. It wasn't until later that I really appreciated why Christian Scripture and Tradition tell us that Jesus is especially present with the poor and neglected of this world. The story goes as follows:

In the basement of my home sits a round piece of flint stone, chipped on one edge. This greyish-brown relic, not quite the size of a baseball, tells a meaningful story.

The stone is an Indian play ball, hundreds of years old, found in a borrow pit (dump). It was buried there generations ago. When looking at it, I reflect on the days when Aboriginal children played with it on the banks of the Miami River, near where it was unearthed.

My memories of the stone shifted recently, as I watched a

commercial soliciting money for disabled veterans. It pictured a veteran with a disfigured face. Then, I remembered the man who sold the play ball to me. His name was Morley.

I can't recall where I first met him, but I'll never forget him. He too had a scarred, disfigured face, resulting from being burnt. Until I saw the soldier on television, I only thought of the play ball and wondered about its value. I never thought of Morley, the man who sold it to me, before I saw the commercial. Then, my thoughts changed. I now think of Morley before I reflect on the ball.

I remember Morley as a man with the most disfigured face I've ever seen, resulting from a fire fight when he served in the military during the Korean War. After Morley incurred his injury and returned from combat, he shied away from people because of his appearance. He lived in a small house near the river. Rarely did he go into town, and he worked at a few odd jobs to support himself.

After I met him, I occasionally stopped at his place, where he sold items that he found when salvaging along the river. That's where he dug up the play ball. As I got to know him and looked beyond his disfigured face, I discovered a wonderful man who spent most of his time alone. Later, reflecting on his countenance, I saw why Jesus was especially loving with the poor and needy.

Thinking about Morley led me to realize that the real value of the play ball is not found in its material worth or scarcity but in symbolizing Morley's struggle to survive after his accident — and in reflecting the disenfranchised Native American people who carved and played with the ball.

In other words, the true value of the ball was in Morley who found it and in those who made and played with it. It reminds me why early Christians were especially mindful of those in need as they gave them their time, friendship, and talent.

Morley's scarred, disfigured face also reminds me of the disfigured Christ on the cross and of our call to reach out to the needy. When we remember Morley's story, let us recall that all of us are broken, as we apply this lesson to our families.

Many broken families exist today. They are beset with many challenges, as were early Christian house churches. The latter faced persecution and rejection from society. Today's church of the home faces challenges of materialism, individualism, and secularism coming through technology, the internet, and society in general.

Faith Formation. Early Christians taught in the temple and in their households. Their commitment to religious instruction was the lifeblood of the early Church, as it was in Judaism. Their role model was Jesus, the teacher of teachers, whose example showed early Christians the way. In their teaching they focused on proclaiming the Good News, moral instruction, and preaching. Their example reminds today's families, especially parents, that every family member influences the faith formation of the entire family through prayer, sacrifice, and good works. Essential aspects of early house churches set the tone for the rest of this book. Before discussing their impact in greater depth, we will consider the post-Apostolic house churches and Church teachings on the family that emerged after Vatican II. These influence the current emphasis on the domestic church.

Questions for Reflection

❑ In reflecting on the Holy Family, how can pastors and other parish leaders more effectively communicate the values of the Holy Family to family members?

❑ What values that the Holy Family exhibited are important for families today?

❑ How can Jesus' genealogies in Matthew and Luke help homilists when dealing with the imperfect condition of people who struggle to do what is right?

❑ How do the struggles of the Holy Family point to the need for an increased emphasis on faith formation today?

❑ How would you, as a pastoral leader, use the elements present in early house churches to motivate parishioners today?

❑ Which elements of the house churches are the most significant to consider in your ministry to families?

❑ How can the Holy Family's life as a healthy yet struggling family assist pastoral leaders when dealing with issues such as a girl pregnant out of wedlock or an alcoholic parent?

❑ What surprised you the most when reflecting on the genealogy of Jesus as applied to your ministry with teenagers?

❑ If you were asked to describe the meaning of the expression *domestic church* in the parish bulletin or on a website, how would you answer?

❑ How can you make the domestic church a greater priority in the parish?

Chapter Three
New Directions in Family Ministry

Don't get bogged down in your own limited ideas and opinions, but be prepared to change or expand them.

Pope Francis, Amoris Laetitia[1]

A historical review of house churches helps us appreciate their significance today. This history began in the house churches that emerged after Jesus' resurrection. Influenced by Jewish tradition emphasizing the home, they incorporated Christian belief into their lives.

We'll limit our study to what is significant in establishing a groundwork for today's domestic church, as we trace a brief history of house churches from post-Apostolic times to the present.

HOUSE CHURCHES IN THE POST-APOSTOLIC PERIOD[2]

After Jesus ascended into heaven, Christians met in house churches during times of persecution and peace. Eventually, rooms were added to larger homes to provide adequate assembly places for Christians to gather for hospitality, prayer, and celebrating the sacraments.

After AD 312, when Constantine permitted Christians to celebrate their beliefs freely and openly, larger churches were constructed. After this happened, gradually the house churches ceased.

From the beginning, Church leaders stressed the significance of baptism as the foundation for the Christian life and for Church membership. They recognized that the Christian family had an ecclesial nature. To deepen the connection between family and Church, St. John Chrysostom (347–407) and St. Augustine of Hippo (354–430) compared the father's role in the home to the bishop's role in the larger Church. For example, Augustine said that good bishops and fathers of a family serve Christ by living upright lives, giving alms, and proclaiming God's word. The father of a household gives affection that he owes his family and teaches, encourages, corrects, gives warnings, shows kindness, and exercises discipline. Consequently, "in his own house he will be fulfilling an ecclesiastical and kind of episcopal office."[3]

St. John Chrysostom called the Christian home a *little church*, whereas St. Augustine used the expression *domestic church* or *household church* in referring to the family. In their writings, they indicate that the Christian home has an ecclesial identity.

St. Thomas Aquinas (1225–74) and other Church leaders in the Middle Ages spoke of the sacredness of marriage, comparing the union of man and woman to the union of Christ and his Church. They spoke of the chief role of marriage as the procreation and education of children, which the Council of Trent (1545–63) reiterated. Until Vatican II, this was understood to be the primary end of marriage. The Second Vatican Council put an equal emphasis on the mutual love of the spouses, showing that marriage has two purposes. The theology of the domestic church existed in latent form throughout the centuries, but Vatican II brought it into a new light.[4]

VATICAN II

The seeds for developing an ecclesiology of the domestic church were sown in the documents of Vatican II. This began when the Council shifted the orientation of the Church from a perfect society or institution to the People of God. This is found especially in chapter two of *Lumen Gentium*,[5] which stresses the Church as the People of God. It set the stage for acknowledging the Church as primarily a community of believers, not an institution. As a believing community, the significance of relationship and evangelization has taken on a new emphasis within the Church and rests on what Pope Francis calls *engagement*. With community in a prominent place, the Church has recognized the ecclesial nature of the family and its significance as a domestic church.

This did not happen all at once. It took years for the Church to see the wide-ranging implications of the shift of focus from institution to community and its ramifications for the family. This happened concurrently with a greater appreciation of the role of the laity and the role of Christian discipleship that took shape in the minds and hearts of Catholics.

Bishop Pietro Fiordelli played a prominent role at Vatican II in seeing the family as a domestic church. At first, the Council Fathers did not recognize the significance of his recommendation. In referring to the family as a small church, he brought to light the ecclesial nature of the family. Eventually, *Lumen Gentium* described the family as being regarded as the domestic church.[6] It took time for the Church to recognize the ecclesial implications of this statement. Even though this language was used, the ecclesial relationship between Church and family was not developed.

Pope St. Paul VI in *Evangelii Nuntiandi* enhanced the Church's teaching on the ecclesial nature of the family by speaking of the family as a domestic church.[7] Succeeding popes accepted this description as the foundation for their pastoral care of the family. The family is now recognized as the smallest organic cell in the Church. How this gradually happened is described below.

NEW DIRECTIONS FROM CHURCH DOCUMENTS

In focusing on the Church as a community of believers, new pathways opened up for a deeper understanding of relationships in marriage and the family. Describing the family as the most intimate of communities offered new insights on various facets of the family. No longer was the primary end of marriage described only in terms of the procreation and education of children. Begetting and educating children in the Faith are important aspects of marriage, but equally significant is the mutual love of the spouses. After Vatican II, both ends of marriage, grounded in Christ, were seen in a new way.

In relating the family to the domestic church, *Lumen Gentium* established the groundwork for looking anew at the family, based on insights gleaned from early house churches. In this, the family is critically important in what it means to be a church. As noted above, this new appreciation of the family, rooted in communion ecclesiology, developed slowly. As it did, new directions based on Vatican II teachings emerged from papal statements, Church documents, and pastoral theologians.

To better appreciate these insights when relating the family to the domestic church, we'll consider several documents — namely, *Evangelii Nuntiandi* (Pope St. Paul VI); *Familiaris Consortio* and *Christifideles Laici* (Pope St. John Paul II); "The Prayer and the Holy Family of Nazareth" (Pope Benedict XVI); *A Family Perspective in Church and Society* (NCCB, 1998); *Amoris Laetitia* (Pope Francis); and the *Directory for Catechesis* (Pontifical Council for the Promotion of the New Evangelization).

Evangelii Nuntiandi (Pope St. Paul VI)

The focus on the family as domestic church goes hand in hand with a new appreciation of every Christian's role as an evangelizer. The Sacrament of Baptism roots the Christian call to evangelize. It sets the foundation for viewing the Church as a community of believers and the new People of God. In *Evangelii Nuntiandi*, Pope St. Paul VI brought these teachings into light. This apostolic exhortation has been called the "Magna Carta of the New Evangelization." In it, the pope relates evangelization to Jesus, the great evangelizer, and describes the call of every Christian to evangelize or to proclaim God's word. This can be applied in a unique way to parents.

Catechesis, liturgy, and service ministries are aspects of, or moments in, the evangelization process. Initial acts of evangelization, missionary work, catechesis, and ongoing pastoral activities are unified under the banner of evangelization. In this context, the role of the Christian disciple, beginning in the family, is to evangelize. Missionary discipleship begins in the home.

Familiaris Consortio (Pope St. John Paul II)

Following the teachings of Pope St. Paul VI, Pope St. John Paul II reemphasized the family in his apostolic exhortation *Familiaris Consortio*. In the preparatory work for the synod that led to this document, representatives from Western nations spoke of qualities of marriage such as intimacy and relationship. Third-world representatives took a different focus, stressing that their primary concern within family life was survival — food and shelter — not intimacy. This discussion indicates the significance of culture in dealing with evangelization and the family, which was taken up in *Familiaris Consortio*. It established the groundwork for a deeper analysis of family differences among various cultures.

In *Familiaris Consortio*, Pope St. John Paul II points to the value of the family in the Church and the world. He describes the family in personalistic terms as a "communion of persons"[8] living together in a complex web of interpersonal relationships. In these relationships, children witness their first experience of the Church. In relating with each other, family members participate in an "itinerary of faith,"[9] a path in which they relate to God and the broader Church community. In this web of life, all Christians are called to evangelize.

Comparing the family to the broader Church, Pope St. John Paul II calls the family "an intimate community of life and love,"[10] gathered together to love and support each other and to participate in Christ's mission to proclaim the Word to all nations. Families participate in the Church's mission by evangelizing, relating as a community with God, and serving the needs of others. The pope's teaching builds on post-Vatican II directives regarding family members being ministers of evangelization, as he describes the priestly, prophetic, and kingly functions of the family.[11]

Familiaris Consortio sets the foundation for acknowledging the family as a domestic church and gives more specificity to the elements of family life that connect the family to the parish and broader Church. For pastors and pastoral ministers, this document is a strong incentive to place greater emphasis on the family as a domestic church.

Christifideles Laici (Pope St. John Paul II)

As Vatican II gave increasing clarity to the family as a domestic church, another affirmative step forward happened with the publication of Pope St. John Paul II's apostolic exhortation *Christifideles Laici* in 1988. The subtitle summarizes the contents of this work on the Christian laity: *On Vocation and the Mission of the Lay Faithful in the Church and in the World.*

The laity's mission is alluded to throughout this publication. Pope St. John Paul II wove his comments on the laity around a Scripture passage from Matthew: "go into the vineyard" (Mt 20:1–16). In so doing, he illustrated the increasingly important role that the lay faithful play in the missionary activity of the Church.

The document stressed that the call to mission is not just for clerics and consecrated religious, but it is the vocation of every baptized Christian. Never before had the dignity, spirituality, mission, and responsibility of the lay faithful been emphasized as in this document. To reinforce this statement, the pope described the priestly, prophetic, and kingly function of the laity, as rooted in baptism.[12] Then, he referred to the Second Vatican Council's emphasis on the mystery of communion as focused on the laity. This ecclesiology of communion set the groundwork for what Pope Francis would later say about the need for engagement, dialogue, and interpersonal relationships when dealing with the family as a domestic church.

Pope St. John Paul II linked missionary activity with the responsibility of parents and family members to regard their family as a domestic church, arguing that going into the world as workers, business managers, technicians, teachers, and a multitude of other roles is the proper missionary activity of the laity. This enables family members to recognize their unity with the diocese and universal Church in proclaiming Jesus' message.[13]

As the primary cell in the Church, the Christian family is at the heart of all pastoral efforts to evangelize culture. This begins when parents strive to make the family a domestic church, for Christian missionaries are first formed in families, before going into the wider Church and world. The family is the natural school of formation in the Faith.

"The Prayer and the Holy Family of Nazareth" (Pope Benedict XVI)

As Christmas approached in December 2011, Pope Benedict XVI, in a general audience, stressed the importance of prayer in the home. Calling the house of Nazareth a "school of prayer," the pope indicated the significance of prayer in striving to make the home a domestic church. Describing the roles of Mary, Joseph, and Jesus, he stated: "Jewish families, like Christian families, pray in the intimacy of the home but they also pray together with the community, recognizing that they belong to the People of God, journeying on; and the pilgrimage expresses exactly this state of the People of God on the move."[14]

Being on the move is an apt expression today, with people living at a frantic pace. For this reason, it is imperative that the family prays together in the fast-paced lives that they live. Pope Benedict XVI concluded:

> Because of these different aspects that I have outlined briefly in the light of the Gospel, the Holy Family is the icon of the domestic Church, called to pray together. The family is the domestic Church and must be the first school of prayer. It is in the family that children, from the tenderest age, can learn to perceive the meaning of God, also thanks to the teaching and example of their parents: to live in an atmosphere marked by God's presence. An authentically Christian education cannot dispense with the experience of prayer. If one does not

learn how to pray in the family it will later be difficult to bridge this gap. And so I would like to address to you the invitation to pray together as a family at the school of the Holy Family of Nazareth and thereby really to become of one heart and soul, a true family.

The image of the Holy Family as an icon of prayer encompasses the Holy Family's faith, which Christian families are to emulate as a domestic church.

A Family Perspective in Church and Society (NCCB)

This document, first published by the United States Conference of Catholic Bishops in 1988 and subsequently revised in 1998, refers to the family engaged in social relationships. It says, "As a systems orientation, a family perspective is a lens that focuses on the interaction between individuals, their families, and social situations."[15]

Following the lead of *Familiaris Consortio*, this document emphasizes the relational aspect of families and recognizes that today's families are faced with impending challenges. It describes the Christian vision of family life, pictures the family as a developing system with a great deal of diversity, and addresses the family's relationship with other social systems.

Recognizing these dimensions of the family is helpful when considering its call to evangelize, for the efforts of family members to evangelize are conditioned by the cultural context in which families find themselves. A similar dynamic existed in the early house churches, where a family perspective was evident.

Evangelii Gaudium (Pope Francis)

In *Evangelii Gaudium*, Pope Francis stresses having a personal encounter with Jesus. Living out the call to Christian discipleship depends on this relationship. Once this foundation is set, families can more intentionally carry out their call as missionary disciples to "[g]o therefore and make disciples of all nations" (Mt 28:19).

These words set the stage for evangelization in the family. Pope Francis indicates that evangelization happens in the simple actions of everyday family life, such as preparing meals, having patience with a child, one sibling helping another with homework, and praying at bedtime with children. Such actions set the stage for deeper, more profound actions later on, exemplified by young family members who stand up for what they believe in and who set good examples for their peers in school or on the playground. With adults, this is manifested by engaging in just business practices and doing volunteer work for the poor.

Pastoral activity is rooted in our relationship with Jesus. The more intentional we make this relationship, the clearer our responsibility for evangelizing activity becomes. This begins in the family, the domestic church.

In *Evangelii Gaudium*, Pope Francis speaks of the current crises in families and the need to remain close to Jesus and the Church. For this generation to respond with pastoral actions in parishes and schools, a Christian's activity must heal, promote, and reinforce personal bonds.[16] When ministry is done in a personal way, culture is evangelized and missionary discipleship happens.

Stressing the missionary role of the baptized, Pope Francis says, "In virtue of their baptism, all the members of the People of God have become missionary disciples. … Every Christian is a missionary to the extent that he or she has encountered the love of God in Christ Jesus."[17]

Amoris Laetitia (Pope Francis)

Amoris Laetitia, subtitled *On Love in the Family* and published in 2016, is the fruit of the bishops' Synod on the Family, held the year prior. In it Pope Francis reinforces his emphasis on family relationships, encounter, dialogue, missionary discipleship, and evangelization. He articulates how each of these personally touch the minds and hearts of family members and are the way of the family, exemplified by the Holy Family.

The pope says, "Every family should look to the icon of the Holy Family of Nazareth."[18] Coupled with the genealogies of Jesus in Matthew and Luke, his words affirm that the Holy Family was a healthy yet struggling family.

The pope also speaks of the essential role of dialogue, especially when things do not go well in family life. He says, "Dialogue is essential for experiencing, expressing and fostering love in marriage and family life."[19] Its importance is reflected in the story of Jesus in the temple. Through dialogue, Mary and Joseph resolved their differences with their twelve-year-old son, after they searched for Jesus and found him in the temple listening to and asking questions of the Jewish teachers (see Lk 2:41–52).

Amoris Laetitia is a wonderfully human description of the joys and challenges of family life in our time of superficial and ephemeral pursuits. In contrast to the impersonal nature of secular culture, Pope Francis speaks of warmth, tenderness, and compassion as remedies for today's secular world.

Pope Francis challenges Christian spouses to live as Christ did by accompanying and caring for their families. This means it is important for spouses to take time to learn and to listen to what the other thinks.[20] Rooted in the Beatitudes, accompaniment is necessary for Christian families to become domestic churches. Parents "are the principal agents of the family apostolate, above all through 'their joy-filled witness as domestic churches.'"[21]

Directory for Catechesis (Pontifical Council for the Promotion of the New Evangelization)

The *Directory for Catechesis*, published in a new edition in 2020, brings into focus the main developments in evangelization and catechesis since Vatican II. It is rooted in the belief that every baptized person is called to be a missionary disciple.

This calling begins in the family's vocation to be agents of evangelization and catechesis. The paths that bring families to this point and their relationships to the parish, diocese, and universal Church are varied, and they will continue as such in our fluid and changing world. But the fundamental ways that this happens are clear and basic. This *Directory* addresses them, and they are included in part two of this book.

Consistent with the personalism of Pope Francis, the *Directory for Catechesis* describes the three basic tenets of evangelization as witness, mercy, and dialogue.[22] In doing so, the *Directory* affirms the emerging belief that if evangelization is to be successful on a wide scale, the Church as a whole and families in particular need to put these qualities at the top of their priority list and reflect them in their family lives, workplaces, and neighborhoods. The world needs food, clothing, and other necessities. In addition, it requires compassionate actions that show mercy and love. It is imperative that the Christian stance be one of listening and dialogue, in order to meet the hunger for meaning that is widespread in society.

Listening and dialogue begin in the family. The *Directory for Catechesis* stresses the significance of parents in mirroring a living faith at home and sharing it with those whom the family touches every day. Pope Francis insists that a culture of inclusion is essential, one that exists in the home and reaches out to the broader society. The age-old word *welcome* looms even larger as the response that Christians first learn in their home churches and then bring to the world. The *Directory* accentuates the need for welcome in its commitment to pursuing an "option for the poor."[23]

Finally, the *Directory* challenges Christians to accept their calling as missionary disciples by engaging in the world of technology and committing themselves to mercy in their efforts to bring life, hope, and compassion to the digital arena.

Questions for Reflection

❏ What standard rituals and prayers were found in early house churches, and what do they tell us today?

❏ Why do you think that St. John Chrysostom and Saint Augustine compared the father's role in the home to the bishop's role in the larger Church?

❏ Why were Vatican II Church Fathers initially reluctant to recognize the significance of the family as a small church? What happened after they changed their minds?

❏ What insights from the above Church documents have influenced you?

❏ How can you help family members or parishioners recognize their roles as missionary disciples?

❏ In speaking of the domestic church, describe parental responsibilities using the categories of priest, prophet, and king.

❏ In giving a homily, how would you see the relationship between a domestic church and the parish church?

❏ Discuss: "The relationship between Gospel and culture has always posed a challenge to the life of the Church."[24]

Chapter Four

Culture, Climate, and the Domestic Church

*Evangelizing does not mean occupying a
given territory, but rather eliciting* spiritual
processes *in the lives of persons so that the
faith may become rooted and significant.*

Directory for Catechesis[1] *36*

Culture and climate play a vital role in forming the religious
attitudes of a domestic church. To gain greater insight into
their influence, this chapter addresses their relationship with the
domestic church and suggests a blueprint for Christian living. I

will begin with a personal story to illustrate the influence of a positive family culture:

When I was five years old, my dad and I returned from a Thanksgiving morning football game at a local high school. We were anxiously awaiting the special meal that Mom was preparing when the doorbell rang. My sister, Mary Ann, and I ran to answer it. Standing outside were a boy about twelve and a girl about nine. The girl carried a baby under a shawl. They said, "We are poor children and have nothing to eat. Will you give us money, so we can buy food?"

Mary Ann and I called our mom, who listened to the children's story. When they finished, she said, "We don't have much money but will gladly share our food with you. Come and join us for Thanksgiving dinner."

The children looked funny and said that they couldn't stay. Mom replied, "Wait here and we'll get some food for you." As the children waited, Mary Ann and I felt good as we helped Mom prepare a meal for each child. We gave them turkey, dressing, cranberries, gravy, potatoes, green beans, and a drink. Mom also put milk in a flask for the baby. The children took the food, but they looked funny as they left. We were happy because we shared our meal with them.

Since it was a warm, beautiful day, my sister and I walked onto the front porch and watched the children go up the street. When they got to the corner, the girl suddenly threw the baby to the boy, who put it under his arm. They continued to throw it back and forth. Finally, with a strange smirk and laugh, the boy pitched all the food we prepared down the open sewer, as the children disappeared around the corner.

While this was happening, Mom came onto the porch and saw the whole thing. Mary Ann and I cried out and kept blurting, "They hurt the baby; they threw away our food."

Consoling us in a loving embrace, Mom put her arms around

us and said, "Bob and Mary Ann, we will have the greatest Thanks-giving ever, and you will learn an important lesson today."

We answered, "How can we? They hurt the baby and threw away our food." Mom replied, "We'll have a great day nonetheless. That wasn't a baby but a doll; the children tricked us. They didn't want our food; they only wanted money."

Then, Mom said something that I'll never forget: "We'll have a wonderful day, because we'll learn a lesson about gift-giving. We gave the children a wonderful gift of our food. The value of our gift didn't depend on whether the children accepted it. It was a great gift, because we sacrificed and gave it with a good heart."

She continued, "That's the way it was with Jesus. He was God the Father's greatest gift ever. The fact that evil men and women rejected him did not make him any less of a gift. So, let's go inside now and celebrate a wonderful Thanksgiving."

This simple story had a profound impact on my values and illustrates how the culture and climate of our home influenced the family. Mom was a powerful evangelizer that day, when she taught my sister and me more about gift-giving than we ever learned in religion books. Let's use this story as a backdrop as we consider the culture and climate of a domestic church and its impact on the family.

CULTURE AND CLIMATE OF THE HOME

Growth in faith in a domestic household always takes place within a certain culture and climate. Some family cultures are conducive to faith; others are not. Beyond the immediate scope of the family, pressures come to a home from without. Before delving into the impact of a family culture, we'll consider what is meant by a Catholic culture and the climate of the home.

Catholic Culture. A family's culture, vital in the faith formation of its members, is the community framework that provides the foundation for a group's attitudes, responses, and experiences. A family's core culture includes the basic way that its members see things, how they act, their value system, their common patterns of meaning, and their kinds of celebrations. For a Catholic family, the core culture includes the essentials of Catholicism, such as the sacraments, Mass, basic beliefs, and papal leadership. This core culture is the same for Catholics everywhere.

Within this universal Catholic core culture, a whole series of subcultures exist. Catholic subcultures exist in different families, for each family has a unique way of being Catholic. Family subcultures are rooted in the basic assumptions of the Catholic core culture, as they are lived out in a given family.

All Catholics have the same basic or core culture, even though their subcultures vary from family to family and from Latino to Black to Caucasian to Asian peoples. Although the core culture underlying every Catholic parish is the same, the subcultures vary. In one parish, the subcultures may include a strong youth culture or a predominately senior citizen culture. A family's culture includes the assumptions, practices, values, and actions that set the foundation for how a given family thinks, responds, and acts. It includes beliefs, ways of acting, ethnic backgrounds, customs, and traditions.

Most family assumptions are unspoken and preconscious. They root the parents' and children's values and beliefs and influence how family members relate to each other and the outside world. From this complex family culture, each member develops a sense of religious identity.

The family culture indicates what is important or significant for family members and helps explain how they act or react in the family unit and beyond. This culture evolves slowly and is difficult to change. If change does take place, it usually happens on the level of climate, not culture.

Family culture blends religious and secular values. Its shape

is the monitor of action and priorities. Often, it is hard to artic-
ulate. Pastors and pastoral ministers need to consider a family's
culture when addressing faith formation issues. Having a good
handle on a family's culture makes it easier to respond to a given
family's needs.

Catholic Climate. The climate of each group or organization is described as its fundamental orientation, style, and spirit.
The climate of every family is different and affects its attitudes
and ways of acting. The climate of the Smith family may differ significantly from that of the Jones family, even though each
professes the same Catholic core culture. A family's climate is
reflected in how family members treat each other and others beyond the family. Their response may be positive and enthusiastic
or negative or indifferent.

Just as the leader of a business organization sets the tone for
how workers respond to their environment, the parents do the
same in a family. If the family's culture can be seen as the *personality* of a family, its climate can be seen as its *mood.*

The family climate includes the shared perception of parents and children as to how things are going in the family. This
climate may be warm and welcoming or cold and unpleasant.
It affects the family unit itself and those in contact with the
family.

When pastors, deacons, or pastoral ministers deal with matters of the Faith, it is important to connect with the culture and
climate of the people concerned, so as to influence them. This
is especially true when the secular culture casts doubt on the
minds and hearts of religious-minded people.

Since the family climate influences the faith formation happening in the home, pastoral leaders are encouraged to learn a
family's climate. It affects the members, regardless of whether
the climate is good, bad, or indifferent.

George Litwin and Robert Stringer[2] of Harvard Business

School have done extensive study of organizational climates in business and how they impact individuals and groups. Their insights can assist us as we look at how family climates influence family members. To this end, they identify certain aspects of a climate which are applicable to families. Among others, these include:

- Structure — family procedures and the overall family atmosphere
- Responsibility — unique tasks and the role of each family member
- Identity — identification of who each family member is in the family unit and broader society, focusing on a sense of belonging
- Reward — acknowledging and affirming family members, especially when succeeding and completing assigned tasks
- Warmth — general feeling of affirmation, love, positive reinforcement, friendliness, and comfort within the family and toward broader society
- Conflict — being fair and open in dealing with and resolving family concerns and problems

As regards Catholic family faith formation, another aspect can be added:

- Catholic — the home itself includes a positive regard for the Catholic Faith and is characterized by regular Mass attendance, daily prayer, symbols of the Faith, children's and adults' catechesis, and rituals such as the Rosary, Advent wreath, and Christmas crib

FAMILY COMMUNICATION

A family's culture and climate develop in the communication of family members with each other. Parents set the tone for such relationships, whether they are deep, superficial, or somewhere in between. The depth of communication in a family culture often depends on the degree that its members, especially the parents, connect their attitudes and actions with core human values and beliefs such as God's existence, active participation in Church worship, social justice, equality, truth, goodness, and beauty. Unfortunately, some families put little priority on such values, favoring instead secular values, such as money, pleasure, material possessions, profit, and earthly achievements.

Culture, climate, and communication are the backdrop of all efforts to address family religious needs. It is important to keep them in mind, for here values are solidified, and identity is established.

Since a family's culture and climate begin in the communication happening between parents, it is appropriate to ask: Is this communication rooted in core values or superficial, functional ones? How well do the two original cultures, coming from the family backgrounds of husband and wife, blend to form a new family culture when a couple marries? When two people marry, they bring both gifts and baggage from their families of origin. These include ethnic, social, and religious similarities and differences, unique family issues, personal attitudes and beliefs, and work responsibilities.

Each spouse comes from a different family culture. When marrying, the couple retains their unique gifts while striving to incorporate them into a new family configuration. This new Catholic home culture and climate begins with the couple themselves and expands to their children as they come along. In this process, prior relationships influence a couple's values, beliefs, and ways of relating after marriage.

When previously divorced couples marry, they also bring into their new relationship psychological and other dynamics from their former marriage, especially if their new family includes children from prior marriages. Something similar happens when children live with one spouse, a grandparent, another relative, or a friend. When a child is adopted, other dynamics enter the new family.

Each situation is unique and influences the culture of the new family and strongly impacts the climate of the newly formed family relationships. To address such situations, communication is central to a family's future success.

From the above, it is easy to see that every family culture is multidimensional, comprised of interwoven relationships. Communication is necessary not only when a marriage begins, but throughout the family life cycle.

COMMUNICATING BASIC FAMILY BELIEFS

Every family has basic beliefs and values. Some are of a spiritual nature; others are not. Usually, they are a blend of both. When differences occur between spouses or family members, basic beliefs and values come into play. Without understanding them, it's hard to maintain solid, deep-seated family relationships. Basic beliefs are at the heart of a family's corporate personality. They undergird family priorities, which often include sports, business activities, education, social expectations, work, and recreation. These beliefs help form a family's culture. The way a family incorporates them into its positive or negative home climate affects the family's overall health. When a family's culture is healthy, it integrates solid beliefs and practices coming from the parents' families of origin or previous marriages.

A family climate is positive when it reflects solid values and beliefs. It is influenced by the family's healthy living environment and balanced lifestyle. This includes meeting each others' material and spiritual needs, having a well-balanced attitude toward money and possessions, agreeing on educational priorities, and spending time together for fun and recreation. A healthy family climate includes solid communication among the members regarding basic values, beliefs, priorities, and ways of acting.

Regardless of the familial configuration, a healthy family climate is rooted in an implicit philosophy of life that the family accepts. Every family has one, even though it usually is not clearly articulated. The most comprehensive family philosophy of life is not an economic, political, social, aesthetic, or ethical one. It is not based on money, status, or power. Rather it centers on spiritual values. Such a religious philosophy of life is all-embracing. It includes everything worthwhile, good, and beautiful, whether this comes from a religious tradition, exquisite art, good ethical conduct, social awareness, or trustworthy leadership. Where a healthy religious philosophy of life exists, family faith formation begins on solid ground. Here, families create a positive climate from which other aspects of family life spring.

PASTORAL SENSITIVITY TO FAMILY COMMUNICATION

Pastoral leadership needs to be sensitive to the dynamics operating within families, regardless of what those are. Thus, for example, in marriage preparation, developing a Catholic culture and climate in the home can form the backdrop for whatever else a parish requires. In this way, Pre-Cana requirements become part of a holistic approach and are incorporated into a parish's overall plan for marriage preparation. In preparing for marriage, it is important to identify the culture and climate of the spouses before they get married. Some elements of their culture of origin may surface by using the FOCCUS inventory or other existing marriage preparation processes.

In preparing for marriage, the couple needs to look holistically at their lives, attitudes, beliefs, and experiences that might influence their subsequent behavior after marriage. In marriage preparation sessions for mixed-religious couples, their similarities and differences in belief need to be addressed, and suggestions should be offered to help them consider challenging issues, such as their children's education in the Faith.

Something similar applies across the board when engaged couples address what it will look like if they take seriously the creation of a Catholic home culture and climate. Such a home environment begins when a couple marries, and it lasts throughout the marriage. Even though a family's culture and climate are two main factors that influence a marriage, often little is done pastorally to help engaged couples address this fundamental aspect of their future family.

Addressing a Catholic family's culture and climate is a vital step to enhancing a family's faith formation. Special emphasis must be given to key moments in family life, such as a child's birth, beginning school, first Communion, confirmation, graduation, sickness, death, retirement, old age, and leaving the home for college, work, or military service. The family's culture and climate change at such key moments. Many families cope well with such changes; others need help. The parish and Christian community can be of great service to both groups.

Leaders of marriage preparation sessions are encouraged to develop a series of questions and processes to identify key elements of family culture and climate as they pertain specifically to both Catholic and mixed-religion families.

A BLUEPRINT FOR CHRISTIAN
LIVING IN SECULAR CULTURE

Having considered communication in family culture and climate, we now look at Christian living in the secular culture, which Pope Francis calls the "culture of the ephemeral." He says that to live Jesus' message most effectively in this culture, we need to live in a personal and dialogical way, or in other words, in "a culture of encounter."

Let's also keep in mind that Pope Francis encourages family members to follow Jesus' example by moving to the periphery and focusing on the poor, disenfranchised, and alienated. He stresses one-on-one dialogue and says that unless the periphery containing the needy members of society is addressed and brought into the center of the Church's ministry, the Christian community cannot be adequately renewed. The same applies to giving special consideration to family members who struggle. This follows from Jesus' teaching about the poor and children. As we listen to Pope Francis's words, we see the value of rooting our faith in Jesus' presence in the church of the home.

To strengthen the domestic church, pastors and pastoral leaders can encourage families to reflect on biblical passages, such as the Beatitudes, that set the tone for a Christian's way of living. Next, they can look at the ephemeral world and focus on the primacy of love, the path of fidelity, and mutual self-giving. Finally, in homilies and other pastoral ministries, they can remind parishioners that spiritual growth is a dynamic yet gradual process, based on living the Commandments, practicing the virtues, and praying for the gifts of the Holy Spirit.

Families are to consider: What does it mean to live the Christian life in today's world? Put simply, this means following Jesus' lead in a secular environment that threatens to engulf them. The path Jesus walked offers a blueprint for Christian living, as Pope Francis lays out in *Amoris Laetitia*.

At its roots, Pope Francis implies that this blueprint has a fourfold, interrelated dynamic. It includes being (1) welcomed into the Christian world; (2) supported along the way of faith; (3) taught to get along by loving one another; and (4) incorporated into a Christian community. From life's beginning, this fundamental Christian orientation forms the basis for who we are and how we act.

As Christian believers, this blueprint is rooted in divine grace, given at baptism, and continued through life. Pope Francis bases this path of fidelity on the primacy of love as it "is experienced and nurtured in the daily life of couples and their children."[3] In so doing, the pope encourages Christians to live and act as Jesus did.

The four interrelated dynamics, mentioned above, begin with the relationship with our parents and family. Pope Francis says they include a sense of welcome, accompaniment, discernment, and integration, described below.

Welcome. The domestic church is born when a couple marries. From this time on, spiritual seeds are to be planted which help parents develop a faith-filled home. Beginning with initial marriage preparation, a parish can encourage couples to accept the seriousness of their task to bring the Faith to their children. Parents are to be reminded when children enter their world that they are helpless and totally dependent on their parents. What happens in the first months of life plays a vital part in whether children feel welcome or at home in this world.

Affiliation, meaning "unity in close contact," describes the bonding that first takes place between a child and one's parents.[4] Just like a child needs to feel welcomed into life, so also a Christian family needs to make its members and guests feel welcomed in a home that follows Jesus' path of love. Pastors and other pastoral leaders can encourage parents to respond to God's love and forgiveness through the life they live as a domestic church.

Jesus offers us a roadmap, as he himself gathered his followers and asked them to follow him. In this way, he gives families a path to walk as a domestic church. He welcomed his early followers, inviting them to follow him (see Mt 16:24), and he reached out to welcome the paralytic (Mk 2:2–12), the woman at the well (Jn 4:1–30), and the good thief on the cross (Lk 23:32–43). Following in Jesus' footsteps, Saint Paul encouraged the Christian community at Philippi, whom he visited, to welcome his companion Epaphroditus with the words, "Welcome him then in the Lord with all joy" (Phil 2:29).

As in Jesus' time, *welcome* is essential for conversion to happen. Pastors and other pastoral leaders can encourage parish members to link it with the virtues of hospitality, patience, and prudence. *Welcome* sets the foundation for family members' responses at home, in business, or in the marketplace.

Accompaniment. As they grow, children rely on their parents in small and big matters. Put simply, parents accompany them as they learn the basics of living, attending school, becoming active in social work, playing sports, and growing in faith.

Like their parents, children need to learn how to live by Jesus' message. A Christian culture and climate, experienced in the home, assists them in this venture. From it they learn that following Jesus means praying, being kind to others, playing fair, acting justly, honoring God, and telling others about their Faith. In this regard, pastoral leaders can encourage them to give good example to their family and friends, so that their peers see Christ in their actions. Pope Francis would include supporting children in their faith growth under the expression *accompaniment*.

Accompaniment is a key to Christian living. Biblical passages describe how Jesus accompanied his followers as they listened and learned from him. Jesus' actions presume a culture of encounter, a willingness to dialogue and to walk with others in good and bad times.

Pastors and pastoral ministers can demonstrate the importance of accompaniment, beginning in childhood and lasting a lifetime. They can also stress the virtue of patience, reflect on the time that Jesus spent with his followers, and highlight the fact that he forgave them when they betrayed him.

Discernment. As children grow, they learn from their parents. They teach their children to do mundane things, such as brushing their teeth or washing their hands. In addition, they introduce them to a Christian lifestyle of prayer and good works.

Teaching children the beliefs and rituals of the Faith is a necessary aspect of being a responsible Christian parent. Even more important than words is how parents teach their children through their actions and guidance. From parental examples, children first learn to discern what is right and wrong and how to form their consciences.

Jesus laid the foundation for the process of discernment by his teaching, sending the Holy Spirit to enlighten us, and establishing his Church as a guide. In discerning the correct path to take, calling on the wisdom of the Holy Spirit is essential.

Parents need to know what is right or wrong as they accompany others on their faith journeys as spouses, parents, counselors, or friends, especially in moral matters. Families are encouraged to focus on the virtues of faith and hope as they strive to follow Christ and accompany others.

Integration. From the beginning of children's lives, responsible parents make sure that they feel welcomed and part of the family. Integration into family life and helping children see that they are an essential part of it means that children are loved for who they are.

Besides feeling part of the domestic church of the home, children also need to feel connected with the parish and the larger Church community. Feeling part of the family begins in relationships at home. In homilies, pastors, other priests, and deacons can integrate the wisdom contained in the post-Pentecostal Church with living the Christian life in the domestic and parish church. Just as Jesus welcomed his followers into the Church that he established, so also can pastors remind parishioners that everyone living in domestic churches is welcome in the parish.

All the baptized belong to the Body of Christ, a mystical communion centered around Jesus' love. As members of his body, family members can reach out and welcome those who feel cut off from the Church.

Being part of a faith community is vital, for it helps ensure a well-balanced life in a society geared toward individualism. Christians need one another. Pastors are encouraged to stress this, as they recall Pope Francis's focus on the primacy of love, the virtue needed to make others feel welcome and part of the parish community. Often, a loving welcome is the first step toward full integration into the parish.

In summary, as families reflect on Christian life, they are encouraged to remember Pope Francis's four pastoral dynamics: welcome, accompaniment, discernment, and integration. These offer a healthy process for the domestic church to follow. Welcome is the underlying perspective. Accompaniment happens as family members support one another. Discernment occurs as families help one another understand God's will for them. Integration takes place as parents integrate their children into the family's faith.

Family members can remember these four dynamics of welcome, accompaniment, discernment, and integration with the acronym WADI. They invite families to move from a dry riverbed of secular life to the living waters of a stream suffused with the power of the Holy Spirit. In so doing, they strive to be merciful to the poor, needy, and hurting, remembering that the Holy Spirit directs them as God's humble servants.

With the foundation set in part one of this book, we now move to the heart of being a domestic church. We will begin with insights gleaned from early house churches and then use them to address today's domestic church.

Questions for Reflection

- ❑ By what beliefs did your family of origin live? Where did Catholic belief and practice enter your family of origin's culture?
- ❑ As a parish leader, what can you apply to your ministry, gleaned from your early upbringing?
- ❑ How would you identify the five top priorities in your family of origin's culture? Do they enhance or distract from your approach to parish leadership, and why?
- ❑ In discussing the domestic church, why focus on the Catholic climate of the home in your pastoral ministry?
- ❑ What baggage from the past interferes with the positive climate of your approach to family ministry? What cultural factors most influenced your family of origin?
- ❑ What values are most important in your pastoral ministry to families?
- ❑ Discuss whether faith is central or peripheral to the family activities and lifestyles of your parishioners.
- ❑ Reflect on whether preaching on the importance of prayer in family life is a priority in your homilies.
- ❑ How does your parish address the issue of Catholic Faith formation?
- ❑ How would you judge the faith of families in your parish, including frequent Mass attendance, prayer, religious symbols in the home, and such?
- ❑ What does the faith of families in your parish say about the cultures of families in the parish?

PART TWO
FORMING DOMESTIC CHURCHES

Vatican II set the stage for the prominence of the domestic church. Since Bishop Fiordelli first described the family as a small church, a steady development of this concept has taken place in the Catholic Church.

As noted earlier, after Pope St. Paul VI addressed the domestic church in *Evangelii Nuntiandi*, the use of this term became more common in Church teaching and pastoral documents. Every pope after him added to the ecclesiology surrounding it. Church leaders increasingly stressed the family as a domestic church and its relationship to the parish, local, and universal Church.

As this happened, pastors and other Church leaders began incorporating a family perspective into homilies and parish activities. They recognized that the family was not a ministry among other ministries but an essential aspect of the Church. This led to more fruitful marriage preparation and the growing realization that the family is at the heart of what it means to be a parish.

Today's Catholic Church is at a crossroads. The time has arrived to delve more deeply into the theology of the domestic church and implement new insights derived from seeing the family as a domestic church. Family stories have a way of putting such insights into proper perspective. One story, gleaned from a treasure trove of my personal memories, reflects an important aspect of our family's domestic church:

When I was a boy, our family owned a small dry goods store in the West End of Cincinnati. It was a happy place where neighborhood folks laughed and cried together. People bought merchandise there, knowing that all poor black, brown, and white people were welcome.

In early December, a delegation from the black Holiness Church came into the store and asked to talk with my father. When they left, he told me they invited him to preach the Christmas sermon at their church. "Dad," I asked, "what did you tell them?" He replied that he wanted to talk it over with Mom before giving them an answer.

I sensed what his decision would be — that the only sermon he could preach was in the store. The following Thursday, he walked up the street to tell the church members that he couldn't do it. He returned shortly, hoping they understood.

Two weeks passed, and on the day before Christmas, Dad found out how well the people understood him. The church people came into the store carrying chicken dinners — a delicacy they occasionally brought us on busy days. Dad was overjoyed. As he thanked them, we gathered around the old potbelly stove. Dad threw in several large lumps of coal. The warmth of Christmas Eve melted the chill in the store as everyone laughed, reminisced, and ate their chicken dinners.

Before they left, Dad picked out a nice selection of gifts, clothes, and household items for the church's poor who might not receive much on Christmas Day. As the coal turned to ashes, the black and white brothers and sisters exchanged best wishes for peace, joy, and goodwill around the old stove and preached the real Christmas sermon.

The old store and church are gone now, but memories live on. Whenever I drive past the spot where the store once stood, I remember that special Christmas that taught me the real reason for Jesus' birth.[1]

This story serves as an introduction to part two of this book, which addresses key aspects of family faith formation. It includes stories of the early Church, especially Jesus' life and the lives of Christians who formed the first house churches. This section of the book is rooted in God's call to every baptized person to be a missionary disciple, like my dad in the story. It consists of six chapters that discuss key elements in family faith that flow from the call of every Christian to proclaim the kingdom of God, and it suggests insights that arise from the early house churches.

These chapters begin with the importance of relationships in our lives and end with the call to faith formation. In each one, personal stories and the current situation in society invite us to bring Jesus' message into our families and work. As a prelude, we begin part two with the call of the disciples and then focus on the Beatitudes, using them to set the overall direction for each chapter.

Jesus called Peter, James, and John while they went about their ordinary work as fishermen. Fluffy words meant little to such hardened, tough men. Knowing this, Jesus literally got into the water and mud with them as they slushed around in the Sea of Galilee.

After Jesus gained their respect and showed them his power through the miracle of a large catch of fish, he invited them to follow him (see Lk 5:1–11). Imagine the magnetism of his personality! These strong men left the only profession they knew to follow him, thus risking their livelihoods and the security of their families. From the beginning of his public ministry, Jesus taught his followers to rub shoulders with those they hoped to influence.

Words and prayers were not enough. Jesus' way of relating to his followers reminds pastors and parish priests to examine their approach to ministry and make sure they are not personally or liturgically aloof from parishioners, thus failing to effectively communicate with them. This happens whenever Church leaders lose the pulse of the people whom they are sent to serve.

Like Jesus' early followers, today's Christians must connect the flesh and blood of everyday living with Jesus' teachings. This happened in his time, as he gradually formed the minds and hearts of his disciples. It continues today when Christians follow the Lord and accompany the joyful and hurting members of his Mystical Body. This is a gradual process and requires patience.

The early Christian community never demanded that new members be perfect before they embarked on their journeys of faith. Like Jesus, it welcomed sinners and encouraged them to become saints. It has to be the same now, as pastoral ministers encourage parishioners to live like Jesus did.

When Jesus formed his initial band of followers, he addressed their doubts and uncertainties about who he was and what his mission was. On one occasion, he spoke to a large group of followers and curious bystanders who followed him up a mountain. Here, he preached the Sermon on the Mount.

Imagine what it was like as Jesus climbed the mountain with his chosen followers, prior to addressing the crowd! What did

Peter, James, John, and Mary, his mother, think when they saw throngs of people from the surrounding countryside, villages, and towns struggling to get close and listen to him?

Jesus' charismatic presence motivated the crowds to endure the sweat and heat of that arid place. How many Roman soldiers were there? Were they sent to keep tabs on him? While there, did they discover a deeper meaning, beyond what they experienced in the military? Did the poor and destitute, present that day, hope for a miracle that might cure them? How many believed that Jesus was the longed-for political Messiah, sent by God to free the Jews from captivity by the Romans? Did some attendees wonder if Jesus would inaugurate his kingdom by calling his followers to begin a battle with the Romans who kept them in submission?

Regardless of their hopes and desires, Jesus surprised those who followed him up the mountain by proclaiming a kingdom radically different from the one they anticipated. The Gospel of Matthew says:

> When Jesus saw the crowds, he went up the mountain; and after he sat down, his disciples came to him. Then he began to speak, and taught them, saying:
>
> "Blessed are the poor in spirit, for theirs is the kingdom of heaven.
> "Blessed are those who mourn, for they will be comforted.
> "Blessed are the meek, for they will inherit the earth.
> "Blessed are those who hunger and thirst for righteousness, for they will be filled.
> "Blessed are the merciful, for they will receive mercy.
> "Blessed are the pure in heart, for they will see God.
> "Blessed are the peacemakers, for they will be called children of God.

"Blessed are those who are persecuted for righteousness' sake, for theirs is the kingdom of heaven.
"Blessed are you when people revile you and perse-
cute you and utter all kinds of evil against you falsely on
my account. Rejoice and be glad, for your reward is great
in heaven, for in the same way they persecuted the prophets who were before you." (5:1–12)

The disciples who heard these words were steeped in the Ten
Commandments and the Torah, but Jesus' words went beyond the
law of Moses. In his teaching, Jesus affirms his Hebrew faith in one
God and professes his belief in the law and the prophets. But he
does more, as he changed the focus of the crowd's concern for a
Messiah who would free them from subservience to the Romans.
To their surprise, he mentioned nothing about Roman rule. Rather, he taught that the heart of his kingdom is not about overcom-
ing a strong military power, or class warfare, or anything else that
pertains to material accomplishments.

What, then, did the Beatitudes teach the crowds? How many
understood their true meaning, even though Jesus couched them
in ancient Jewish beliefs? How would they affect their lives? Did
anyone wonder what Jesus' words promised for living a virtuous
life?

Similar questions need to be asked today. What do the Beatitudes mean for us? Are they pious words that we hear in Church,
or are they more? They may comfort us in funeral liturgies and
make us feel good when we serve the poor, but what else? In our
secular, materialistic world of relative values, greed, and waste,
what meaning do they have?

The Beatitudes fly in the face of modern consumerism, secular technological advances, and an amoral world that has little
regard for modesty or the need to moderate human desires. They
provide a largely untested spiritual roadmap, offering a new direc-

tion for a fresh way of life. They are the foundation for family faith formation. Pastors and pastoral ministers are invited to address their importance as they minister in Christ's name.

The Beatitudes were at the heart of early Church belief, as Jesus' disciples met in their house churches. They contain the core values of virtuous living, at variance with the priorities of a worldly society. Jesus' words reflect themes that the major world religions profess; for example, the noble eightfold path of Buddhism and the Islamic teaching on fasting, prayer, and almsgiving.

Early Christians centered their lives on the Beatitudes, Jesus' formulae for righteous living. When lived by families and other parish members today, they become the leaven that spreads the Gospel through secular society. If this happens, the external world may look the same, but Christians working in the world and living by the power of the Gospel will change it from within.

This happened in Jesus' time. After Pentecost, his followers reflected on the Sermon on the Mount in light of his resurrection. They learned its true meaning as they integrated the implications of his dying and rising into their lives.

A Beatitude is quoted in the beginning of each chapter that follows. In reading it, keep in mind that Pope Francis reiterates again and again that every baptized person is called to follow Christ as a missionary disciple, regardless of one's state in life. He stresses that professing faith in Jesus Christ requires that we accept him as our personal savior, desire to learn from him, and give witness to Beatitude values through our actions.

For this to happen, words alone do not suffice, for homilies and catechesis by themselves are not as effective in moving people's hearts as is the human face of Jesus, brought alive in faith-filled Christians. Such testimony is the foundation for virtuous living in our secular, materialistic, and amoral world. Such a witness provides the basis for a revitalized Christianity in the world of computers and social media.

For Christians to live as missionary disciples in our materialistic society, discipline is necessary. This hit home to me when I was teaching a Comparative Religion class for students from poor and inner-city families. They knew the scourge of poverty, had experienced gang warfare in the streets, had seen shootings and muggings, and had felt the challenge of single parenthood — especially of single motherhood — often with five or more children.

During one class, I asked whether young people and adults need discipline to live righteously. Without equivocation, they said yes. Then, they began discussing the strict rules and obligations of some religious groups in the area who were attracting young men to join them. The students said that these groups are attractive because young people look for discipline and a roadmap to follow. "Unfortunately," one student remarked, "mainline churches have become too soft."

Comparing mainline Christian norms of fasting with the stricter practices of some non-Christian religions, they chuckled. Another student said, "How can a person develop a disciplined, stable way of life by fasting a couple times yearly and occasionally saying some prayers?" After she said this, others discussed effective ways to fast to bring one's body into line with one's soul.

Reflecting on the value of discipline and fasting in a me-centered world makes us wonder whether sacrifices to control one's body and feelings are taken seriously. How many people freely sacrifice food, drink, or time if there is not something in it for them? How often do we reach beyond ourselves to share what we have with others? How many really hear Jesus' words: "Repent, for the kingdom of heaven has come near" (Mt 4:17)?

The discipline necessary for true Christian love is intimately associated with living the Beatitudes and with fulfilling Jesus' great commandment to love God and our neighbor. In Matthew, we read, "'You shall love the Lord your God with all your heart, and with all your soul, and with all your mind.' ... And a second is like it: 'you shall love your neighbor as yourself.' On these two commandments hang all the law and prophets" (Mt 22:37–40).

The early Church realized that self-discipline and following the Commandments are prerequisites for living the Beatitudes. They recognized the significance of Jesus' suffering and death on the cross and its impact on their lives. In so doing, Jesus' first followers looked to him as their model. They remembered how he prepared himself by fasting and prayer to accept the ultimate destiny that his Father ordained for him as the Savior of the world. The sleepless nights, concern about his disciples (in particular their seeming difficulty in understanding his teachings about giving of themselves), the many days spent fasting, and his hours in prayer prepared him to undergo the final trial of his suffering and death.

In the pain that he endured, Jesus steeled himself for his final ordeal, so that as he sweat blood in the garden, he had the courage to cry out, "My Father, if this cannot pass unless I drink it, your will be done" (Mt 26:42), rather than to leave and run like his disciples.

When looking at the Beatitudes in light of Jesus' death and resurrection, it became clear to the early Church that no Christian can live the fullness of the Beatitudes without having courage and mastery over oneself, brought about by the practice of self-denial and personal discipline. All the Beatitudes presume a degree of mastery over oneself. If this is absent, they are pious words but not faith in action.

Seen in this way, "blessed are the poor in spirit" is more a process of learning how to live a life of self-abandonment than of carrying out any single act of mercy. To master oneself takes years; so does learning how to be merciful. As we move into the wisdom learned from the early Church in the rest of this book, the Beatitudes provide a backdrop for faith and become God's lifeline to happiness.

Questions for Reflection

❑ How can parishes increase their efforts to help parishioners recognize that they are called by Jesus through their baptism, as the early disciples were called by Jesus?

❑ How can pastors and pastoral teams encourage parents to help their children see their important role as followers of Jesus? Give specific examples.

❑ How can pastors and other parish leaders use the Beatitudes as a formula to teach and equip families for righteous living in their homes?

❑ How do the Beatitudes provide an overall orientation for a missionary disciple to follow?

Chapter Five
The Call to Relationship

*Blessed are the poor in spirit, for theirs
is the kingdom of heaven.*

Matthew 5:3

In every family, relationships among family members and relationships beyond the family are critical. Deep relationships
profoundly affect our faith and are the foundation for missionary discipleship.

This chapter stresses the significance of relationships and
their influence on a family's role in following Christ. We begin
with early Christian disciples, consider how their mutual relationships were the basis of their house churches, and provide a

fresh perspective for domestic churches of the home. Saint Paul testifies to this in his address to the Thessalonians when he says, "We must always give thanks to God for you … because your faith is growing abundantly, and the love of every one of you for one another is increasing" (2 Thes 1:3).

After Pentecost, Christians banded together, often in households, to support one another. They formed deep relationships that enabled them to grow in faith and to follow Christ's call by proclaiming the Word. As a motivator of their actions, they realized that Jesus' words, "Blessed are the poor in spirit," challenged them to give of themselves, even to the point of death.

Their way of being poor in spirit still rings true, for giving of oneself is vital for relationships to deepen and bear fruit. In their busy days, pastors, parish priests, and other Church ministers can be mindful that faith and self-sacrifice are at the core of following Christ. It's worthwhile for them to recognize the graced moments that are a golden thread keeping them connected with the God they serve.

A relationship with God and our Catholic Faith was important in my family growing up. We shared it with each other and with our friends. A strong influence on my faith happened when I was sick as a young child. Here is part of my story:

From our earliest years, my parents set a family tone which reflected our Catholic Faith. We lived across the street from Saint William Church, and many conversations dealt with what was happening there. As we grew, our relationships with family members and neighbors testified that we were Catholic.

We attended Church services regularly, played on the Church grounds, talked to the priests and nuns, and gave witness to our Faith with friends and neighbors. Religious statues were in our yard and in most rooms of our house. We lived in a Catholic climate.

In good times and bad, our parents' example at home testified to our Faith, sustained us, and gave us hope. I especially remember when I began the first grade.

Shortly after school started, I became ill. After a doctor thoroughly examined me, he determined that I needed absolute rest for a whole year. After he said that I would have to miss the first grade, my mom asked him if she could teach me what the other children were learning in class. The doctor said that would not hurt me, if she wanted to try. Mom spoke to the nun who taught the first grade at Saint William School and got permission to teach me.

The memory of that year is vague, but what remains embedded in me is how Mom gave of her love and sacrificed for me. I remember that each day she faithfully walked across the street and spent considerable time with the first-grade teacher finding out what the children in my class had learned that day. Then, she came home with books in her arms and taught me the lessons of the day.

I also recall how Mom taught me to pray, be patient, and make the most of our time together. During that year, a powerful bond formed between us that lasts beyond her death. Our relationship made a huge difference in my life, especially in my faith. During good and difficult days, who Mom was to me influenced strongly who I became. Our relationship set the foundation for everything else in my life.

That year, Mom instructed me on how to read, write, and be a faithful Catholic. Near the year's end at Eastertime, after I got stronger and returned to school, I was two weeks ahead of the rest of the class.

Even though Mom taught my lessons well, I learned more from her kindness and love than from any book. Her simple gestures of love indelibly imprinted on me the right thing to do and set my value system on the right path.

I never found out what was wrong with me, but whatever it

was turned out to be a blessing, as I established a lifelong bond with my mother that served as the foundation for who I am and what I became.

When I reflect on the relationship between Mom and me, fostered during that year of sickness, I recall the importance of all family relationships. Many are positive; some are not. In this regard, Pope Francis says, "There is no stereotype of the ideal family, but rather a challenging mosaic made up of many different realities, with all their joys, hopes and problems."[1]

These words remind us of the Holy Family, a healthy yet struggling family. Like all families, they experienced joys and good times, as well as struggles and disappointments, in their relationships with one another. Struggles came from without, such as the flight into Egypt, and from within, such as the disagreement that happened when Jesus was lost in the temple at the age of twelve. Other events occurred in Jesus' life that remind us of the importance of communicating effectively in family relationships during good and difficult times.

For this reason, we'll now consider Jesus' relationships with his disciples and then look at relationships in early house churches.

JESUS' RELATIONSHIPS WITH HIS DISCIPLES

When we consider Jesus' relationships with his first disciples, questions enter our minds. Why did ordinary fishermen and a tax collector leave their work and families to follow him? What motivated holy women and sinners alike to become his disciples? This happened not only because of what he said and did, but because of who he was.

From Jesus, the early Church realized the power of relationships and how they set the stage for Jews and Gentiles alike to listen and respond to the first Christian evangelists, as they proclaimed his message. This is important for pastors, deacons, and other pastoral ministers to consider as they evangelize in the parish and beyond it.

While reflecting on relationships among Jesus and his disciples, we imagine the close relationships he had with John, Mary Magdalene, Peter, and others. They were deep and ultimate testimonies to who he was. We remember also the relationships with those with whom Jesus worked as a carpenter before he began his public life. These were functional relationships entered into in order to get a job done.

In recalling Jesus' relationships, we recognize that he had two kinds: ultimate and functional ones. Functional relationships are impersonal and objective; ultimate relationships are personal and subjective.

As I sit at my desk, I have a functional relationship with my computer, the paper that I use, and my printer. In these functional relationships, I treat what I use as things. These are objective, impersonal relationships. On the other hand, I have an ultimate relationship with the person to whom I write. Ours is a subjective or personal relationship.

In our highly sophisticated society, many daily relationships are functional. They begin with relationships in our home. Much of what we do there is functional and impersonal. This includes keeping the house in order, preparing meals, doing homework, and more. In such a world, it is often challenging to develop and maintain ultimate relationships. These require time and effort and are at the heart of living.

When we speak in this chapter of relationships, we refer to ultimate ones. Jesus' followers came to faith through interpersonal relationship with him. It is the same with us. We come to faith through the deep love of our parents, siblings, children, and faith community, not primarily through objective words in a catechism.

Faith formation operates primarily on the level of ultimate

relationships. For this reason, pastors and other pastoral ministers are encouraged to examine the kinds of relationships that they have with parishioners. Are they functional or ultimate relationships? Do they manifest a sense of welcome, care, and concern?

RELATIONSHIPS IN EARLY HOUSE CHURCHES

The ability to relate to one another sets the stage for listening to what is said. This happened after Pentecost as Jesus' early disciples remembered his Last Supper, suffering and death on the cross, glorious resurrection from the dead, and appearance to his followers before he ascended into heaven.

Appreciating Jesus' love opened them up to accept the call from the Holy Spirit to follow Jesus and be part of the Christian community. Their faith and love of one another changed them and the world. When early Church members, such as Peter and John, spoke sincerely and honestly, nonbelievers listened.

Such relationships were paramount for early disciples who committed their lives to Jesus. The Acts of the Apostles says, "Now the whole group of those who believed were of one heart and soul, and no one claimed private ownership of any possessions, but everything they owned was held in common" (Acts 4:32).

From these words, we infer that community relationships and sharing with each other were basic modes of living. Even when the disciples disagreed, they listened to what the Holy Spirit was saying to them through openness and dialogue. What kept the Christian community of one mind and heart? It was the conviction that Jesus, the crucified one, was raised from the dead to testify that he is the Son of God. As Acts says, "With great power the apostles gave their testimony to the resurrection of the Lord Jesus" (Acts 4:33).

When thinking of the relationships among the early disciples of Christ, I recall a story that reminds me of what those relationships might have been. The story is about Jake, a poor man like many of Jesus' followers:

When I was a boy working in my father's store, I met Jake, a man who gave the impression that he really cared for others. He lived in a tenement house and had recently moved into the neighborhood from the Appalachian Mountain region of Tennessee. From the time that I met him, his goodness and calm demeanor impressed me. We never spoke about religion, probably because Dad told him that we were Catholics.

After about six months, I heard that Jake had left the area to become a preacher in a small evangelical church. He had little learning but preached his beliefs largely by his actions.

As a young person, I never understood why other poor people flocked to Jake's church to hear his message of love. Later, I realized that they listened to him because he lived what he preached. In his simple way, Jake cared about them and developed personal, ultimate relationships with them. Consequently, they followed him.

In some ways, Jake reminds me of the early disciples of Jesus, many of whom were unlettered, as Jake was. His story reflects a quality of compassion for all pastors and parish ministers to emulate. Objectively speaking, Jake's understanding of the Bible was limited, but the words he preached were uttered with conviction and an ultimate sense of purpose. I see in him what Pope Francis stresses about relationships as setting the groundwork for Christian calling.

What I witnessed as a boy in Jake, the preacher from Appalachia, can equally apply to relationships in a domestic church or ministry in a cathedral. The word of God must be lived and be spoken with conviction in a personal way, so that Jesus' message comes alive in our time, as it did when Jesus walked the earth.

Would that this be a priority for all family members and pastoral leaders!

MISPLACED RELATIONAL PRIORITIES

When I think of the need to establish relational priorities in family living, I remember an episode that occurred while I was teaching a college class, an episode that was at variance with the personal qualities manifested in the story of Jake:

We were discussing relationships and the importance of communication in the family. The allure of money raised its head during a class discussion of priorities in marriage. I asked the class, "From your vantage point, what will be your first priority: your job and making money, or growing in relationship with your spouse and children?" The class was divided, but most agreed that spending time communicating with the family was more important than making money. One young man, however, vehemently disagreed. He opted for the functional and chose making money. He said, "For the first five years of my marriage, I intend to put my time and energy into making money at my job. Then, after I am secure, I'll use the money that I made and devote myself to my relationship with my wife and kids." After he ended, I thought, "By the time you make your money, your wife and kids may no longer be around." He gave little thought to working together with his spouse to establish priorities. His self-centered approach reflected the individualism that often is seen today. His attitude was a recipe for disaster.

FAITHFULNESS IN RELATIONSHIPS

During the trials and tribulations of Jesus' difficult life, he never wavered but remained faithful to his mission. Such faithfulness existed in my childhood with my father and mother, who accepted the challenge to care for my brother and sisters, as they did for me. This began with their wedding vows and lasted a lifetime.

Parents today strive to do the same but are under a great deal of pressure. They work hard to make ends meet, raise their families, and provide a good home for them. As they do so, they realize the importance of keeping their lives in balance, ensuring that functional things do not take precedence over deep and loving relationships, which take time to develop. Such loving relationships may require a parent, at times, to spend long hours with a struggling or sick child, like my mom did when I was sick. Nothing else could have substituted for her care.

Parents have a lifetime to get it right. When they fail on this or that occasion, they can correct their ways of acting if they reorient their lives to make it happen. When it comes to a choice between loving relationships and making money, ultimate decisions must always come down on the side of relationships.

Thinking about the vital role that loving parents play in the growth of children can lead some couples to refocus their present relationships, especially if fidelity in marriage is lacking. Some couples live together but never marry, others shirk their responsibility to raise their children in the Faith, still others have extramarital affairs and are not faithful to each other. On the other hand, most spouses are faithful and do their best to love each other and their children.

When considering parental fidelity, we must keep in mind that the responsibility to provide a good home includes more than spouses being faithful to each other and providing material things. A teacher recently told me: "Parents often give their children many things. In so doing, their relationship with them can become functional, even when they attend their sports activities or other endeavors. They give their kids a lot, but what children really need is love, which sometimes is absent. Children crave affection and want to spend time together with their parents."

Relationships develop over time. It took years for the disciples to form a deep-seated community with Jesus and to recognize him as a spiritual Messiah. No matter how hard he tried, while he was alive they never understood that he was not a political Messiah who would conquer the Romans. It took his crucifixion and resurrection for them to finally see his true role. During their years together, however, he planted the seeds that came to full bloom after Pentecost.

Something similar applies with family relationships. We often take our families for granted and in life's ordinary ups and downs fail to appreciate how we incorporate elements of our family relationships into how we deal with others. This usually happens in the simplest of ways. Here are a few episodes from my life:

My sister, Mary Ann, and I, as four- and five-year-old children, often waited on the corner of Sunset and Saint Williams Avenues to see our dad coming home from work about 5:00 p.m. When we saw his car coming down the street, and he got to the corner and stopped, we ran as fast as we could on the sidewalk down Sunset Avenue to see if we could get to our house before he did.

I also recall our family's Sunday drives to Harrison, Ohio, to get an ice cream cone and meet my grandparents there. Our relationships were solidified through these ordinary ventures and the time spent with our loved ones. Relationships, formed in such ways, last a lifetime.

Simple stories like the ones above indicate the significance of relationships in family faith formation. They influence our ways of dealing with our friends, neighbors, work associates, and others that we meet.

RELATIONSHIPS AND COMMUNITY SUPPORT

Healthy relationships in a family are enhanced by support from the larger community. After Pentecost, community living was vital for Jesus' followers. They realized the importance of being together for mutual support, prayer, and fellowship. The Acts of the Apostles says:

> All who believed were together and had all things in common; they would sell their possessions and goods and distribute the proceeds to all, as any had need. Day by day, as they spent much time together in the temple, they broke bread at home and ate their food with glad and generous hearts, praising God and having the good-will of all the people. (2:44–47)

The emerging Church discussed what Jesus taught them in addition to proclaiming the Gospel to society. Their newfound faith was a joy, and daily they appreciated the tremendous gift that God gave them in the person of Jesus and in the Faith they now professed. Through prayer, instruction, time spent together, worship in the temple by early converts from Judaism, and celebrating Jesus' resurrection on Sunday, they received new insights into the paschal mystery.

The joy they celebrated was highlighted each Sunday when the followers of Jesus assembled to celebrate Jesus' resurrection. These meetings nourished and prepared them for the ordeals they faced from an alien world, especially when persecution came. The disciples' commitment to the Christian Faith inspired others to join them, as Acts says, "And day by day the Lord added to their number those who were being saved" (Acts 2:47). Conversions abounded, and many of Jesus' followers sacrificed their lives, rather than reject him.

Just as community was essential for them, so it is for today's Christians. Challenges and troubles are different from what early Christians encountered, but they still exist. This is especially true for young people, who may be ridiculed for attending Mass on

Sundays or going against social norms on moral matters. The path of the Christian is never easy, and living out Christ's message may involve sacrifice, rejection, and ridicule. In facing such challenges, active community participation is necessary.

Positive faith reinforcement begins at home. In vibrant domestic churches, parents and children alike support one another and set an example for others to follow. Pastors can encourage parishioners to give thanks for their families and discern ways to support one another in having fun, in recreation, and most importantly in prayer. In so doing, families set the tone for facing the challenges of the secular world, where they spend most of their time.

When early Church members associated with one another, disagreements arose. Some were intense, and we learn from how Saint Paul responded to them. This is reflected in his First Letter to the Corinthians, where he reminds the disciples to be of one mind and heart. He says, "For it has been reported to me by Chloe's people that there are quarrels among you, my brothers and sisters" (1 Cor 1:11). After reminding them that they belong to Christ, Saint Paul says, "For as long as there is jealousy and quarreling among you, are you not of the flesh, and behaving according to human inclinations?" (1 Cor 3:3).

These words of Saint Paul are a perpetual reminder that families are human, and disagreements will happen. They occur even in the closest families. Seeing family life, however, as a domestic church, we are reminded by Saint Paul's words to be open to communication and dialogue, which can resolve our disputes.

It is sad when conflict occurs in a family. How much better when family members communicate effectively with one another, even when they disagree, rather than separate from each other because of unresolved disputes! This came home to me when my mom and I were at a farm auction:

As we approached the crowd attending the auction, we

sensed tension in the group. Since we knew no one there, we paid little attention to what was happening until it became apparent that cherished items were being sold for much more than they were worth.

Four or five people were competing for certain family items, paying high prices as they bid against each other. As this was happening, a woman next to us said, "Isn't it awful what's going on? They should know better."

When she realized that we didn't understand her, the woman continued, "Years ago, a rift occurred in this family, and the children opposed each other. It became so intense that they refused to communicate. After their mother died, the conflict continued, and they could not agree on how to divide up the property and belongings. So, they decided to have an auction. Did you notice how high the bidding went? They are bidding against each other, trying to keep one another from getting the prized items. How terrible!"

In a short amount of time, many nonfamily members left, while the family siblings continued their efforts to prevent each other from getting what they desired.

This event remained in Mom's and my memory. We often spoke of it. I wonder if Saint Paul had something like this in mind when he upbraided the Christians in Corinth. Family disagreements are inevitable, but moving beyond them and seeking reconciliation is the true path of a domestic church.

Questions for Reflection

❏ What is more important for parishioners: a kind, compassionate pastor, or one who is a good administrator with poor interpersonal skills? Discuss.

❏ Do most families focus on functional or ultimate relationships in their daily communication and activities with family members? How does your answer affect the tone of your preaching and your approach to pastoral ministry?

❏ What time in your life did you experience true faithfulness from another family member? How does its memory assist you in your pastoral ministry? How did it affect your faith?

❏ What simple actions from your family, when you were a child, affected your future way of thinking and acting as a priest?

❏ What event or events in your life profoundly influenced your growth in faith?

❏ Why is it important for a pastor and other pastoral ministers to stress with the parishioners that healthy family relationships strengthen children's growth in faith?

Chapter Six
The Call to Accountability, Hospitality, and Evangelization

Blessed are those who mourn, for they will be comforted.

Matthew 5:4

After Pentecost, the small band of Jesus' followers grew, motivated by their conviction that Jesus continued to live and minister through them. The disciples accepted their calling in ways they never anticipated. They preached the Lord crucified and risen, as Jesus commanded them before he ascended into

119

heaven. His words, "Go therefore and make disciples of all nations" (Mt 28:19), were their rallying cry.

Imagine what it was like when they faced the power of the Roman empire and perdured! A grace-filled conviction that they were sent by Jesus enabled these simple, ordinary people to band together and form a Church that was accountable for spreading Jesus' teachings.

ACCOUNTABILITY

The once fear-laden apostles and disciples, who denied Jesus and ran away during his crucifixion, became powerful witnesses of his resurrection. Consider the scene after Pentecost in the Acts of the Apostles, where we read, "Now when they [Jewish leaders] saw the boldness of Peter and John and realized that they were uneducated and ordinary men, they were amazed and recognized them as companions of Jesus" (Acts 4:13).

Nothing stopped Peter, Paul, Mary Magdalene, John, James, and the other apostles and disciples from proclaiming that Jesus is the Messiah, prophesied in the Old Testament and sent by God to redeem the human race. They suffered flogging, imprisonment, persecution, torture, and death. As their suffering intensified, their faith inspired others to take up the cross and follow Jesus.

What supported them and gave them courage? It was a special gift of the Holy Spirit, moving them to profess their faith. But it also included the spiritual support received from other Christians in prayer and worship in the temple and from their mutual encouragement in house churches, especially on Sundays, as they gathered to pray and celebrate the Eucharist.

When reflecting on today's domestic churches, what would happen if Christian parents stressed to their children that a major aspect of their lives includes being accountable to share Jesus' message of love and forgiveness, as the early disciples did? In other words, what difference would it make if they taught their children from their earliest years that their lives involve living out and professing that Jesus is Lord and that they are missionary disciples in a Church that carries this message to the world? Family life would change if such accountability became a top priority. Pastors, parish priests, and deacons have many opportunities to share this message with parents from the pulpit and in other priestly activities. For such accountability to happen, parents need to embed this truth deeply in their hearts.

HOSPITALITY

All humans have an empty spot in their hearts. We sense it when we feel lonely, lost, or abandoned. It affects some more than others. Even in good and prosperous times, when our hearts burst with joy, we feel a tinge of sadness as we realize that those good times will not remain forever as long as we live on earth.

This hole in our hearts hints that more is to come after this life. But while we live here, we will experience that something is missing. This is the result of original sin, the cause of our feeling lost or incomplete. Our good and bad actions attempt to fill up this incompleteness.

Living by faith helps us strive for completeness. It intensifies our vibrancy as faith-filled Christians and members of a community. It includes the hospitality and welcome spoken of in our parishes but seldom realized in a full manner.

We are accountable to God for our hospitality to others, especially to the needy. Hospitality, a matter of the heart, is an effective way to fill up our hollowness, regardless of our age or state of life. An excellent way to grow a parish is to offer hospitality in all its vigor. This means convincing parishioners that the entire community is to welcome its members and visitors, especially the poor and disenfranchised.

Such hospitality is first learned in the home. As a matter of the heart, it fills up the empty spots, whatever their cause may be.

Pastors and pastoral staffs can encourage parishioners to stress the welcome that every family member needs to feel, as reflected in Josh's story:

A teacher named Maria told the story of Josh, a young boy who came from a good family that was active in their parish. Josh had four brothers and sisters.

Externally, all seemed fine. Josh was no problem in school. In fact, Maria complimented Josh's parents on his behavior at a parent-teacher meeting.

As Maria and Josh's mother became better acquainted, the boy's mother told her that he was a problem at home, often acting out. This surprised Maria, and she accepted Josh's mother's invitation to visit their home to see for herself.

When Maria arrived, Josh greeted her, but soon it became apparent to her that his younger brother was the mother's favorite. Maria watched as Josh's mother upbraided Josh for going outside and not communicating with his brothers and sisters. At dinner, she moved him and gave the favorite spot next to Maria to her younger son.

Afterwards, the parents got together with Maria. She told them that Josh's acting out seemed to be in direct response to how they neglected him and preferred his younger brother.

Surprisingly, the mother did not realize what was happening. Soon, the family began counseling. Josh's attitude eventually changed, as his parents really welcomed him into their family. Before that, the hole in his heart was too big to fill, so he acted out.

Josh's story indicates that hospitality begins at home as a matter of the heart. From there, it extends outward to the parish and neighborhood.

As members of Christ's body, we bring something to every relationship. Sometimes our kindness and welcome helps fill up the hollow spots in people's hearts. This happens in a variety of ways. Parents do so by manifesting their love for each other and their children. Parish leaders do so by extending welcome to all parishioners. As Saint Paul says, "[It is such] love that comes from a pure heart, a good conscience, and sincere faith" (1 Tim 1:5).

Love for one another moves family members to ask, What do I bring to the relationships in my family? If our dealings are limited to what fosters functional relationships, such as money and earthly possessions, this is not enough. Any true gift is rooted in something deeper such as love, concern, forgiveness, or compassion. When these are priorities in a relationship, material gifts symbolize something deeper. When ultimate relationships are missing, functional gifts mean less. Only ultimate gifts, such as love, satisfy the needs of the human heart.

EVANGELIZATION

Hospitality, a special gift, reaches a fuller expression when the Holy Spirit, through the Church, welcomes us to come and be with Jesus. Theologically, we call this divine welcome *sanctifying grace*.

The Church, beginning in the domestic church, provides the Christian climate for divine grace to flow. Grace is a gift of God, and the Church is the channel for supernatural graces that bring divine friendship. This happens when someone is baptized, and it continues as parishes celebrate the sacred mysteries that make Christ present among us in the Mass and other sacraments. Families are vehicles of God's grace when they welcome friends and guests in the spirit of Christ, and parishes do so when they open their arms in the spirit of Christian love.

Together, the family and parish work to fill up in their members the hollowness inherited from original sin. In filling their hearts with love, families and parishes prepare themselves to share God's blessings through evangelization. They do this as missionary disciples when carrying out Jesus' injunction to teach all nations.

The *Directory for Catechesis* describes evangelization as "an ecclesial process, inspired and supported by the Holy Spirit, through which the Gospel is proclaimed and spread throughout the world."[1] Evangelization speaks about something that Christians have always done, as they proclaim the life and teaching of Jesus, celebrate the liturgy, and assist the needy and poor.

Evangelization is a new word for an old reality, for Christians always shared their faith. This began in the early Church and continues today. Just because the Church did not formerly use the word *evangelization* does not mean that it never occurred. From the beginning, it was a vital part of the Church's mission.

When considering evangelization and the directions arising from Vatican II, my thoughts go back to the early days of my priesthood, reflected in the following story:

The summer of my first priestly appointment in 1960 as an assistant priest was a relatively easy one. I had plenty of time, which the pastor soon recognized. One day he said, "Bob, often parishes take a census of their parishioners. We did that a few months ago and came up with a list of inactive Catholics. I would like you to visit them and encourage them to return to active church attendance."

This I did. My visits revealed reasons why they left the Church and what we could do to encourage them to return. It was the first time I realized that to evangelize required us to take people where they are and go from there to effectively share God's word. This insight was my first step on a long quest to find new ways to evangelize, ways that would be effectively employed. I never used the word *evangelization* that summer, but that is what I did as I walked from house to house.

This story brings home what Pope St. John Paul II meant when he said that the new evangelization is not a new theological proclamation, unheard of before this time. The word of God remains unchanged, and it is the same today as when I visited the people on the list that my pastor gave me during the first year of my ordination.

With that said, something about the word of God is new. What is it? It involves the culture in which it is proclaimed. Culture constantly shifts, so God's word must be applied to new circumstances. In so doing, the unchanging word of God is ever new in its application.

This newness comes from how the word is applied to changing times and situations. I saw this when visiting the fallen-away Catholics on the list that the pastor gave me. Put simply, this means recognizing where people are on their faith journeys and using this knowledge as a starting point to accompany them on the road to conversion. When the word of God is applied to the current times and circumstances, what comes from this dialogue will be ever new.

The *Directory for Catechesis* makes this point, saying, "The Church finds herself facing a 'new stage of evangelization' because even in this change of era the risen Lord continues to make all things new."[2] Then, the *Directory* continues, "The Holy Spirit is the soul of the evangelizing Church. For this reason the call for a *new evangelization* has less to do with the dimension of time as with making all moments of the process of evangelization ever more open to the renewing action of the Spirit of the Risen One."[3]

The "ever newness" of God's word is illustrated in the domestic church of the home. The way God's word is applied today differs from when I was a child. At that time, the word was applied in a culture where people had no televisions, computers, or cell phones. We were lucky to have a radio and a party line phone in our house. Most families had one or no car, and the streetcar or bus was the ordinary means of transportation. Active membership in the parish was a vital aspect of our lives. Life was simpler then, even though we did not consider it that way. It was the way that things were.

Today, life is different. In the future we will look back and consider current devices, practices, and ways of living outdated and out of touch. That happens as change occurs ever more rapidly. In every context, the word of God is ever new, with fresh applications needed. This is especially true within families. Parents need to be tuned into the current culture and apply God's word in a meaningful way. This requires solid instruction and clear insights from Sunday homilies at Mass. This challenges pastors, priests, and deacons to make new applications of the word to parishioners' lives. As technology advances, it also means that parents and families need solid Catholic teachings coming not only from parish catechetical sessions, but also from the internet. When the culture changes, so does the methodology of evangelizing Catholics and the broader society. Digital technology is a useful way for this to happen.

In this regard, the *Directory for Catechesis* says:

> The relationship between Gospel and culture has always posed a challenge to the life of the Church. … In the current situation, marked by a great distance between faith and culture, it is urgent to rethink the work of evangelization with new categories and new languages that may serve to emphasize its missionary dimension.[4]

In this context, evangelization means "eliciting *spiritual processes* in the lives of persons so that the faith may become rooted and significant."[5]

Relating the word of God to the culture is no easy task. This begins in the home, especially in relationships that family members have with each other and in how they assimilate their faith into everyday living. Starting with parents, the domestic church is challenged to be accountable for ensuring that Jesus' way to salvation is included in the culture of the family and its dealings with the outside world. This is emphasized by Pope Francis, as he addresses missionary discipleship, the focus of chapter seven.

Questions for Reflection

❑ How can pastors encourage parishioners to be more accountable for ensuring that their families learn their responsibilities as missionary disciples?

❑ How can pastoral ministers remind parishioners not to favor one child over another, thus making the child who is less regarded feel unwelcome?

❑ Why do pastors and other pastoral leaders need to apply the word of God to current times and circumstances so that what comes from this dialogue will be ever new?

❑ Why does relating the word of God to the culture begin in the home, especially in family relationships?

❑ How do pastoral ministers help families assimilate their faith into everyday living?

Chapter Seven
The Call to Missionary Discipleship

Blessed are the meek, for they will inherit the earth.

Matthew 5:5

M issionary discipleship is the Christian's response to the call to evangelize. It was the response of the early Christian disciples, and it is our response as well. This response is effective when it addresses the deepest questions of the human heart, such as: What is the meaning of life? What is the purpose for my existence? People during Jesus' time, through history, and today ask such questions.

When I worked with indigenous tribes in North America, I learned how their young people addressed fundamental life questions before entering adulthood by searching for answers in a vision quest. Many young men went into the forest or a remote place to undergo an initiation rite into adulthood. Supported by a tribal elder, they sought a vision or path forward with the advice of a guardian spirit. They asked for wisdom about their futures, including why they were here on earth.

As I learned more about vision quests, I recalled an event in my life from when I was seventeen. It happened on a beautiful spring day as I walked home from high school. Suddenly, a bright beam of sunlight flashed through a large tree to my left. As this happened, an inner voice said, "I have something important for you to do with your life."

That is all I heard, but this episode remained deeply embedded in my memory. It was a vague but clear indication that I had a purpose in life. Only later did I connect the episode with the indigenous search for a vision quest. Then, I realized that what I experienced on my way home from school was my vision quest. It has taken the rest of my life to discover what the "something important" means for me.

My story fits into the religious rituals of various times and places that tell people that they have something important to do with their lives. In other words, everyone has a mission to accomplish. For the Christian, this includes following in the footsteps of Jesus as a missionary disciple.

Pope Francis emphasizes that missionary discipleship, as it pertains to a Christian's responsibility, comes from baptism and applies to the family as a domestic church.[1] Today, the family's role as missionary disciples is different than when I was a boy. Then, the call to be a missionary was limited to men and women who left their homes to teach nonbelievers about Jesus and win converts to the Catholic Faith. In the early years of my schooling, the teacher took up a collection to send to the missions to gain the souls of "pagan babies" for Jesus.

This approach was based on a different theology of mission, one centered on missionaries from religious communities. Little thought was given to the ordinary Catholic as a missionary in his or her home, neighborhood, or workplace.

Belief in the call of every baptized person to be a missionary in everyday life is a new concept, one often misunderstood by churchgoers. Little do they realize that missionary discipleship was at the heart of what it meant for the first Christians who assembled in house churches. Today, pastors and pastoral teams are entrusted with the privilege of teaching parishioners their role as missionaries, beginning in the home.

In focusing on the family as a domestic church, Pope Francis stresses that all family members are called to be missionary disciples. At the beginning of a couple's preparation for marriage, they can be led to see this as their proper role from the outset of their marriage. This becomes an important foundation for developing a solid attitude about their family. This is articulated in Pope St. John Paul II's *Christifideles Laici* and in Pope Francis's *Amoris Laetitia*. When parents accept their role as stewards of their baptismal calling to mission, they can more easily put other pieces of family life into place. This calling to missionary discipleship begins with them and reaches out to their children.

All family members, regardless of their age, can take up this call to follow Christ in their homes, neighborhoods, and workplaces. When doing so, let them remember Pope Francis's words, "Evangelization takes place in obedience to the missionary mandate of Jesus."[2] To help this happen, pastors, priests, and deacons must support families through their preaching and ministry, encouraging them to be missionary disciples.

A SPECIAL CALLING

My story about the voice and light shining through the tree is everyone's story. Every Christian is called to a special role in life — each different, some more unique than others, but all intended by God to make the world a better place. For Christian missionary disciples this means following the command of Jesus to teach all nations. To better appreciate this calling, let's consider the relationship between our life of faith and the culture where we find ourselves.

LIFE OF FAITH AND CULTURE

In times past, we learned how to be good Catholics at home and in religion classes. Learning the truths of our Faith was relatively simple, as we studied from the *Baltimore Catechism*. Each day, the nun teaching our Catholic class gave us an assignment from the *Baltimore Catechism*. We went home to study it, and our parents heard our homework to make sure we learned it. The next day, we went over it in class.

This method was effective because our home, friends, and Catholic school reflected a strong Catholic culture. This Catholic environment made possible the effectiveness of this mode of learning about our Faith. In contemporary language, Catholics were missionary disciples in their homes, neighborhoods, and workplaces, using their gifts within this culture.

Often, our eighth-grade class gets together for a reunion. We recall this environment and how it inspired us to do what was right, to attend Mass daily, and to believe firmly that the Catholic Church is the true Church. We never called ourselves missionary disciples, but that is what we were.

Today, this Catholic culture in the home has weakened. When it diminished and ceased having a strong influence over its members, the manner of Catholic instruction changed. This change has consisted of recognizing that commitment to the

Catholic Faith, as a way of family life, needs to be *intentional*. In other words, Catholic parents and their children must deliberately decide to be faithful Catholics and missionary disciples.

Simply put, a Catholic couple (or one of the spouses, in the case of a mixed-religion marriage) must intentionally choose the Catholic way of life for their family. This book does not address the issue of faith practice in a mixed-religion family. For information on this matter check my book *When a Catholic Marries a Non-Catholic* (Franciscan Media, 2006). Suffice it to say that whatever the religious affiliation of the spouses, the culture of their family is a vital aspect of faith formation, especially for the children.

The religious orientation of the spouses is a gift they bring to their family. It is an important step along their path of missionary discipleship. Along with other spiritual, emotional, and physical gifts, all family members are encouraged to recognize the Faith as a gift that connects them with the Catholic culture that begins in the family and extends to the world. Being missionary disciples, family members use their gifts to convey the message of Christ as a family and as students, work associates, colleagues, neighbors, and friends.

In our family, my dad used his gifts as a loving father and successful businessman. Mom used her gifts as a loving mother, neighbor, relative, teacher, and friend. Together, they blended their functional gifts with deeper, ultimate ones, such as care and compassion, to make a loving home for our family. They taught us children to pray, practice our faith, and recognize what was right and wrong from their actions at home and in their example outside the home. Their way of raising our family prepared us for missionary discipleship in a new era.

Today, families need to intentionally choose to be Catholics. I see this happening with my nieces and nephews in the changing secular culture where they live and work. Today's parents are challenged to recognize the difficulties involved in being faithful followers of Christ. To follow Jesus' way, as the early disciples did, pastors and other parish ministers can invite parents to make a firm commitment to missionary discipleship, using their gifts to further Christ's mission in a world that desperately needs the values that he teaches.

When parents make a commitment to missionary discipleship, their children can more easily appreciate that they too are called to do the same in ordinary events at home, at school, and in the neighborhood. This does not come automatically, as it once did when the Catholic culture predominated. When parents and children live this way, they fulfill themselves as persons, for Jesus' way is the way God intended for everyone.

In following Christ, missionary disciples face an ever-changing world. Steeped in the present, they look to the future, seek the aid of the Holy Spirit, and need the support of their families and the Church community. For this to happen, parents need encouragement, and young people need affirmation from the pulpit at Mass, parish youth ministry sessions, catechesis, and other ecclesial ministries.

EVANGELIZATION AND MISSIONARY DISCIPLESHIP

Missionary discipleship begins with the witness that parents, families, and Christians give to one another in their homes, parishes, and the broader society. According to the *Directory for Catechesis*, missionary activity is the first stage of evangelization,[3] as it has been from Christianity's inception.

The powerful witness of early Christians caused people in a pagan world to accept Christianity after Jesus' crucifixion. As mentioned earlier, referring to this witness, the Christian writer Tertullian says, "See how they love one another!" The Acts of the Apostles describes how such witness led to the growth of the Church in Jerusalem and other cities throughout the Roman empire.

In their written testimonies, John, Peter, James, and Paul attribute this growth to preaching the word and Christian witness. The good example of Christians opened people up to hear the word of God and to respond. As the *Directory for Catechesis* says, "*Witness* involves openness of heart, the capacity for dialogue and for relationships of reciprocity, the willingness to recognize the signs of goodness and of God's presence in the people one meets."[4] This interaction between witness and proclamation is integral to the ministry *ad gentes*[5] (sharing the Faith with nonbelievers). Serious dialogue with nonbelievers begins when people are open to hear about the Faith and enter formal catechetical instruction.

The call to evangelize brings to fruition the baptismal call of Christians to "go therefore and make disciples" (Mt 28:19). This begins in the home, as parents sit with a sick child, siblings help a family member with chores, or the family reaches out to a poor neighbor. Evangelization for a missionary disciple is a way of life, not an occasional endeavor. It involves the ongoing awareness of what it means to follow Christ.

Pastors and others who work in Church ministry are encouraged to focus parish ministry on helping parishioners recognize the importance of evangelization in the home and, when they have opportunities, to evangelize every day in their technological and digital world. In the parish, this can be done from the pulpit, in parent and catechetical sessions, and during baptismal, first Communion, and marriage preparation gatherings.

Pope Francis stresses dialogue and accompaniment as necessary for missionary discipleship. Dialogue and accompaniment are especially needed in families when members are feeling lonely, looking for companions, joining gangs, or getting hooked on drugs. In such difficult situations, human qualities such as compassion, dignity, intimacy, and mercy must underpin whatever response family members show. Positive attitudes usually engender positive responses. For this reason, Pope Francis describes the value of dialogue, which requires that each person be regarded as an equal, possessing the same rights.

For the domestic church to be a place of warmth and intimacy, accompaniment is essential. This means that regardless of what happens, family members support each other, so that the word of God sheds light on decisions made and actions performed in good and difficult times.

Many people who are doubters, skeptics, or atheists often respond favorably to God's invitation to faith when they witness faith being lived out by Christians. This happened with a former college student of mine:

After attending several introductory classes on Catholicism, Mark stopped me and said, "Father Bob, I really like the way you teach, but I am puzzled by one thing." "What is it?" I asked.

He continued, "Who is this Jesus about whom you speak? Is he still alive?" I was amazed that Mark had never heard of Jesus. We talked at length, and I learned that Mark was a nonbeliever who had no religious background. His parents did not take him to church or mention God at home.

After he entered college, Mark became curious about Catholicism because of the good example of his Catholic friends. Consequently, he signed up for my class. Later, he took instruction and became an active Catholic. The witness of his friends set the stage for him to look more seriously into the Catholic Faith, to enter the Rite of Christian Initiation of Adults, and to become Catholic. To this day, as far as I know, he continues to live his faith.

In family life, the witness and early proclamation of the Faith set the stage for taking it seriously. This happens through good example, formal catechesis, church attendance, and engagement in pastoral activities to reinforce the Faith and pass it on in a formal way. Each of these are a moment in the evangelization process.

In his address during the Angelus on July 15, 2018, Pope Francis offered two aspects of a missionary disciple as an evangelizer.[6] His remarks are significant for parents and families. The first aspect is to make Jesus the center point, or subject, of our lives and all we do. Jesus calls us, and we respond to him. Our life comes from his agenda, not ours.

With this in mind, we can ask: How can parents internalize Jesus' call for them to missionary discipleship? The answer presents a spiritual challenge for parents. The heart of their call to missionary discipleship is to pay tribute to God by doing what Jesus inspires them to do and teaching missionary discipleship to their children, rather than making money or fulfilling a work-related agenda.

In this regard, the second aspect of Jesus' agenda centers around ministry to the poor and disenfranchised. How do parents reach out to them, and how do they teach their children to do the same thing? The poor include the economically, spiritually, psychologically, and emotionally poor. The poor, at one time or another, could be a child rebelling against their parents' faith. The poor can also include a spouse struggling with an emotional issue or a teenager worrying about getting into college.

Pope Francis reminds us that with dialogue as the foundation, Christian missionary disciples can encounter the poor by meeting them where they are, not taking them where we want them to be. Next, it involves accompanying them in their struggles, doubts, or uncertainties. Finally, missionary disciples never give up on the poor but accept them for who they are as they integrate them into a family or parish. Missionary discipleship requires love and compassion, with eyes fixed on Jesus as our center, to guide us through prayer, Scripture, and Church teaching.

Pope Francis's remarks focus on Jesus at the center of our lives and on outreach to the poor. These two aspects of missionary discipleship are the starting point for family ministry, especially for parental response to their call to discipleship.

With these aspects in mind, we observe how Jesus answered his call from the Father. The *Directory for Catechesis* summarizes the distinctive features of his way that consists of "welcoming the poor, the simple, the sinners; proclaiming the kingdom of God as good news; a style of love which frees from evil and which promotes life."[7]

The *Directory* specifies a vital aspect of Jesus' approach, one with profound implications for family life. It says, "Jesus' way of relating to others therefore is distinguished by its exquisitely educational quality. Jesus is able to both welcome and provoke the Samaritan woman in a journey of gradual acceptance of grace and willingness to convert."[8]

Jesus' treatment of the Samaritan woman suggests an approach for every evangelizer, especially parents and family members. The episode shows Jesus' patience and ability to take the woman where she is and gradually lead her to the truth.

How Jesus dealt with the Samaritan woman led her to accept God's grace and the truth. As Jesus had patience with her, so patient waiting may be necessary with a spouse or a child. Authentic Christian discipleship involves accompanying a wayward family member, friend, or neighbor on their journey, providing strength and assistance until the grace of God prevails.

A FAMILY'S CALL TO MISSIONARY DISCIPLESHIP

Taking our lead from the way that Jesus dealt with the Samaritan woman at the well, the following points will help a family enhance their call to missionary discipleship:

- Jesus is at the center of the family, as parents and children strive to be missionary disciples.
- Being a missionary disciple is part of the family's identity, a reason for their existence.
- As a whole and as individual members, families put high priority on the needs of the poor, beginning in the family and extending outward into the world.
- An examination of conscience, included in a family's prayer, asks about their faithfulness to their calling as missionary disciples.
- Family members recognize that whatever good they do is a way to share their call to missionary discipleship.
- Family members assemble on a regular basis to discuss how the family, — as a whole and as individual members — uses their gifts to further the call to missionary discipleship.
- The family recognizes its place in the larger Church, especially the parish, and strives to contribute to its ministry.

Missionary discipleship is not limited to a chosen group in the Church. All Christians receive this call from baptism, and it takes the rest of their lives to live it out. It is not a special ministry or calling but the common heritage of all the baptized. To appreciate it is to appreciate God's presence among us during the joys and sorrows of daily existence.

Missionary discipleship is about developing a new attitude, putting Jesus at the center, and recognizing our special role in building the kingdom of God on earth. It includes giving testimony to our faith. For most of us, this happens in the daily affairs of living. For a select few, it means giving testimony to the Faith as missionaries to unbelievers or to those searching for a formal path to God.

For our purposes, the following testimony of a regular day in the country illustrates how God is present at all times — and how we are called to bring this presence into greater recognition as missionary disciples:

The weather was a brisk seventy-five degrees on Saturday afternoon, with beautiful cumulus clouds interspersed within a blue-tinted sky. After a thirty-minute drive zigzagging through the Indiana hills, not far from the Ohio River, I arrived at my intended location.

As I turned the corner and departed from my car, I recognized members of the family who invited me to their annual summer party. Immediately, I sensed the smell of the roasted corn, chicken, and funnel cakes — symbols of the hope and joy that this yearly event brought to the assembled guests.

As I attended this party each year, I felt a hope renewed when seeing scores of young family members and friends. They symbolized the faith and hard work of those present — and their generosity to neighbors and the needy.

For the family that sponsored this day of appreciation and thanks, joyful and sorrowful stories from the past year brought renewed hope. The yearly celebration was a special day for the younger members to see what living a good and happy life is like. This particular gathering brought joyful and sad moments together, while reminding us of God's presence.

Dinner began with a prayer, as the host remembered those who had died during the past year. Tears flowed down many faces when he read memorials of the deceased. They included family members and friends. A powerful silence ensued as we gave thanks to God for them.

The prayer that afternoon was a wonderful tribute to the love this family and their friends have for God and one another. It brought to a climax the celebration of hope that this gathering affords to the attendees by uniting their sentiments with faith in Jesus. The day reminded us that while we celebrate and have fun with laughter and smiles, we also need support during sickness and death and in life's ordinary circumstances.

Reflecting on the beauty of this afternoon in the country reminds us of the positive role of missionary discipleship. It also helps us to refocus our lives, to appreciate our family, friends, and the blessings of our country, and to ask the Lord to increase our hope in him and trust in one another. In so doing, when difficulty comes, we have the courage to stand strong with faith and love, to thank the ones we love, and to praise the God we worship.

Questions for Reflection

❑ How can pastors and pastoral teams encourage parishioners to consider the implications of seeing that missionary discipleship is the Christian's response to the call to evangelize?

❑ If you heard an inner voice say, "I have something important for you to do with your life," how would you respond? Why do you think that Pope Francis implies that Christian missionary disciples begin by encountering the poor and meeting them where they are, not taking them where they want them to be? What does this imply for pastoral leaders and parents?

❑ How can the conviction that all Christians are called to be missionary disciples help families to refocus their lives and motivate them to increase their hope in God and trust in one another?

Chapter Eight
The Call to the Kingdom of Justice and Peace

Blessed are those who hunger and thirst for righteousness, for they will be filled.

Matthew 5:6

To appreciate the early house churches' motivation for ministry, we remember their ultimate goal was to gain entrance into the kingdom of God. Initially, Peter, James, John, and other followers of Christ preached the kingdom which was intimately related to Jesus' death and resurrection. His coming made possible their entrance into the kingdom, which he spoke of in the

Our Father: "Thy kingdom come" (Lk 11:2).

Jesus was born into a broken world, so constituted after the fall of Adam and Eve. He atoned for our sins, but their after-effects remained in life's struggles and imperfections. Early Christians experienced vulnerability, sickness, death, and persecution. Every person walks this path and decides whether to accompany Jesus on his salvation journey here on earth and in eternal life with God in heaven.

Before discussing the call of every family to share God's kingdom and live justly in this world by following the norms of Jesus, let's compare our world with the past, exemplified by the following scenario:

As I paged through an old book, I came upon a panoramic view of the city of Cincinnati in the late nineteenth century. Looking intently at the picture, it struck me that the tallest, most impressive buildings were the churches. Their majestic spires pointing toward heaven symbolized the faith of the people who built them and worshiped within their walls. These hardy men and women focused on God as the supreme source of their commitment to forge beautiful churches.

Intrigued by this panoramic view of a city dotted with testimonies to the faith of its early settlers, I reflected on other cities of bygone eras — Paris, London, and Rome. In each instance, I recalled similar cathedrals, basilicas, and churches that stand as testimonies of faith. These are often more majestic than those in Cincinnati, many appearing to touch the heavens.

Such places of worship, going back hundreds of years, were constructed without modern means of engineering by people who spent a great part of their lives building them. The pattern of churches, in any city, towering above other buildings was a common one in the past, found around the globe.

With such thoughts in mind, I turned to recent pictures of the Cincinnati skyline, depicting a modern city. Reflecting on them, my mind returned to earlier ones. There is a striking difference.

The tallest churches that once dotted the landscape of nineteenth-century Cincinnati are hard to find, hidden by the larger buildings that now tower over them. The contrast is clear — churches no longer occupy the center of attention in size and magnitude. Instead, other buildings take their place.

Which ones now dominate the landscape? Buildings of prominence now house insurance companies and financial enterprises. In other words, buildings symbolic of worldly affairs — money and finance — have replaced those which once focused on God and higher values.

The changing configurations of important buildings over the span of one hundred years say much about our citizens. Today, major works of architecture — homes or businesses — speak of material wealth, ease, pleasure, security, and success.

What does it say when we put more focus on the security that insurance policies give us than what we receive from an all-loving and trustworthy God? In the current state of affairs, whom do we serve — God or mammon?

The ultimate focus of society has rapidly moved away from God toward material wealth and security. When God is the ultimate focus, everything else fits into place — joy, happiness, suffering, and death. When worldly security and success become our focus, deep values are not adequately addressed. After material success, what comes next?

Slowly, surely, and tragically, in the struggle between religion and secularism, the secular world is winning the day, as it were, without firing a shot. The decline of people attending our churches indicates that Christian word and worship do not connect with many of today's people. As regards the domestic church, more is needed. This is amplified by Archbishop José Gomez' words: "We need to rediscover the radical 'newness' of the Christian message about the family."[1]

We can take our lead from Jesus' teachings, especially his Sermon on the Mount and the Beatitudes. Here, he gave his disciples a blueprint for virtuous living in a secular world. This blueprint is a way of life, embedded in the hearts of those who follow Christ's way to reach happiness and fulfillment. Jesus' public life and teaching on the kingdom of God provide indicators of how his words and actions can touch our hearts and provide the security we need. The Beatitudes offer Christian families new hope in their struggle with secularism, relativism, and the powers of this world.

THE BEATITUDES PIERCE THE DARKNESS

Life in Christ, centered in the Beatitudes, is like an arrow that pierces the darkness of secularism and relativism and offers hope to families and individuals. This arrow brings order from chaos and hope from despair. It offers us renewed energy when we see our existence in light of God's kingdom.

The Christian's deepest energy centers around our belief that God is a God of life, not death. And yet, to walk the path of life, a thousand losses must occur. Jesus' life and death reminds us of this reality. I discovered this in my own life:

In childhood, I cried when my fish died, felt sad when I lost my baseball, and became scared when I was sick. Such little losses were big at the time. When they happened, I lost something that I cherished, but my life went on. This continued into high school. My grandpa's death jolted me. I gave up a college scholarship to go to the seminary and said goodbye to my friends at graduation. Gradually, I grieved these losses and moved beyond them.

It was the same in the seminary, when I rarely saw my family. Yet I went on, realizing that what I gave up was part of a bigger picture that prepared me for challenges in the priesthood.

The pattern of giving up loved ones or personal interests to gain something more continued after ordination. I gave up the joy of married life and experienced a regimented parish life under a strong pastor. I had successes and failures teaching and was exposed to sickness and death as the chaplain of a retirement home.

Early in my priesthood, the changes at Vatican II meant letting go of old ways and welcoming the new. This brought emotional stress and the refocusing of my priorities.

As this happened, following Christ's way of life brought satisfaction when celebrating the Eucharist, baptizing new members into Christ's Body, presiding at weddings, giving spiritual advice, and performing other priestly ministries. Even less gratifying ones like dealing with stressful pastoral situations and tedious administrative functions eventually brought some satisfaction. What I gained put what I had given up in a clearer focus.

Year by year, I saw that striving toward the kingdom of God involves suffering and disappointments — some personal, others professional. The hardest were those associated with the death of my father and mother. In joy and sorrow, I saw that to reach peace and fulfillment means recognizing value in the losses that make possible new life in the big picture of what it means to be human.

The Christian paradigm of joys and sorrows, successes and losses, life and death, reflected in family living, centers around the cross and resurrection of Christ. Human like us, Jesus cried when Lazarus died and celebrated his return to life with Mary and Martha. Seeing family life in light of the kingdom of God, I recognize how Jesus' death encapsulates our losses, and his resurrection invites us to a new way of life after disappointments. As Saint John says, "I am writing you a new commandment that is true in him and in you, because the darkness is passing away and the true light is already shining" (1 Jn 2:8).

From this perspective, hope is the beacon of light leading families forth, and despair has no place in life. Our journey along the arrow of life with its joys and sorrows points to the ultimate prize that Christ won for us — eternal life.

KINGDOM OF GOD

Everyone experiences joys and struggles. The foundation for how we handle them is laid in our families. Parents want the best for their children. They love and support them and work hard to care for them and provide a good home life. They do this due to an inbuilt desire for happiness for themselves and their loved ones.

From a Christian viewpoint, this inner desire is associated with what makes happiness possible. From a faith perspective, the arrow of life from childhood to old age is directed at fulfilling our deep desire for happiness.

Jesus teaches us that being happy is associated with the kingdom of God. Only by following the path that God intends us to take will we reach our final destiny. In so doing, we strive toward the kingdom and fulfill our role through our work, love, and good lives.

When dealing with family matters, the ultimate goal of Christian family life is directed to the kingdom of God. This is the aim of missionary discipleship. To understand what this means for families, we ask: What does Jesus teach us about the kingdom of God?

Put simply, Jesus teaches that God's kingdom is present wherever his divine presence exists. Jesus is the source and the summit of God's kingdom. Furthering it through words and actions is the ultimate goal of Church and family actions. The New Testament teaches us that Jesus' mission was to proclaim the kingdom of God. It is present when family members act as other Christs, in our parishes and in the world. It is present now, but also not yet, for it reaches fulfillment in heaven.

The death of the first martyr, Saint Stephen, manifests God's kingdom. He gave witness to the kingdom of God by his death, offering his life to reveal Jesus' continued presence among us. During his stoning, Stephen said, "Lord Jesus, receive my spirit" (Acts 7:59). Like Stephen, missionary disciples witness the kingdom's presence through their words, prayers, and social concerns.

Jesus' testimony to the kingdom and the witness of the martyrs and other saints through the ages brings hope to struggling humanity. With the promise of happiness now and eternal life to come, hope becomes the virtue of the kingdom, the energy that gets families through difficult times, overcomes brokenness, and promises a new day. This brokenness can be physical, psychological, emotional, or economic. God's kingdom presence can overcome these various kinds of brokenness that humans experience.

As a small child living through the Great Depression in the 1930s, I remember how people struggled *economically*. I also recall the *psychological* toll my father's and mother's deaths took on our family, along with my *spiritual* poverty during a prolonged sickness after an automobile accident. Finally, I witness my *physical* limitations coming from aging. The poverty associated with each situation has been eased by the promise of a new life, if I remain faithful and carry the cross God has given me.

I especially remember how spiritual and psychological brokenness turned into joy after my dad died. As I stood at Dad's gravesite, a large oak tree, a short distance from the spot where I stood, afforded shade and provided a beautiful backdrop for the image of a large crucifix that rested on his grave. The sunlight sparkled through the trees and changed the darkness of the cross to the brightness of a new day.

As I stood at the foot of Dad's grave, a powerful, warm feeling came over me, and I experienced a profound peace. Dad was with me. His body lay at my feet, but his spirit filled my heart. I seemed to hear his voice say, "Bob, I am with God. Be at peace. I will remain with you."

As I looked down at the small flowers that I put on his grave, the sunlight struck them and told me that light overcomes darkness. I felt Dad's presence and didn't want to leave, but I knew it was time to go. I bowed, said a final prayer, renewed my hope, and departed, as the radiance of the day and my inner peace remained with me.

When reflecting on such personal stories, I remember that building the kingdom of God invites us to see that the "triune God is a communion of love, and the family is its living reflection."[2] I remember how Dad reached out to the poor in his small store as a true missionary disciple. Along with Mom, he paved the way for our family to embrace lives of service. They practiced what *Amoris Laetitia* says, namely, "The family is thus the place where parents become their children's first teachers in the faith. They learn this 'trade', passing it down from one person to another."[3]

The United States bishops have prioritized reaching out to the needy by putting social justice high on their agenda. This absolute requirement for missionary disciples is a vital aspect of every domestic church. In my own family, Dad and Mom recognized this in the fiber of their bones, long before they heard of it in Church.

OUTREACH TO THE NEEDY

As Saint Paul concluded his Letter to the Colossians, he told his readers, including "Nympha and the church in her house" (4:15), to "remember my chains" (4:18). These words hint at how Paul suffered during his imprisonment through his fasting, starvation, scourging, and being ridiculed and mocked. He was a symbol for the early Church and for succeeding generations of how Jesus focused on the poor and oppressed.

Paul was admired and followed as a living example by the early Church. As Christians assembled in their homes, we imagine their efforts to reach out to those who suffered like Paul. How they addressed the suffering around them was different from today, but their motivation for serving the needy is an incentive for every family committed to missionary discipleship. With this in mind, the domestic churches need to serve:

- lonely and depressed family members and friends
- sick family members
- neighbors needing financial assistance
- the elderly in our family, among those we know, or in nursing homes
- immigrants and migrants needing assistance
- members alienated from the family
- the homeless and those feeling abandoned
- people with disabilities
- those addicted to drink, drugs, and other things
- people caught in a web of family violence
- women or men suffering from gender inequality
- bullied children and young people

Such people offer domestic churches a focus, pointing to what God calls them to do. It's worth taking time as a family to sift out what kinds of poverty they can address, be they economic, psychological, spiritual, or physical. When helping the poor becomes a priority for families, it is easier to recognize the spirit of Christ dwelling among them.

SOCIAL PRINCIPLES OF THE UNITED STATES BISHOPS

In addition to personal service to the needy, families can address institutional poverty. The social justice teachings of the United

States bishops, applied to families, include the following principles:[4]

- *Life and Dignity of the Human Person.* This is the
  groundwork for all the principles that follow. The
  life and dignity of every person, as equals, is based
  in the belief that all humans are children of God,
  created in God's image. For this reason, every family must strive to remove all prejudice from family
  dealings.
- *Call to Family, Community, and Participation.* Besides being an individual, a person is also a social
  being, needing family and community to survive.
  Families and other human communities have rights
  that must be honored. For children, this means that
  parents are to teach them to treat other cultures as
  equals and welcome them.
- *Rights and Responsibilities.* For persons and communities to flourish, they must be given the rights to
  life, liberty, and justice. These rights bring responsibilities. A family, serving as a domestic church, is to
  make sure that it is sensitive to the rights of those
  beyond their own family.
- *Option for the Poor and Vulnerable.* Jesus put into
  proper focus what is needed for a community to
  survive and grow. This includes giving a high priority to meeting the needs of the poor and vulnerable.
  Families are encouraged to discuss and reach out to
  the needy in their neighborhood or city.
- *The Dignity of Work and the Rights of Workers.*
  Work is honored as one way to continue God's creation. In working, the worker takes precedence over
  the work, for every worker, made in God's image, is

to be respected. Children in families are encouraged to discuss how construction workers, manual laborers, and other workers continue God's creation.

- *Solidarity.* All humans, equal before God, are to be regarded as brothers and sisters. Such equality sets the foundation for supporting the needy and standing with them as they seek equality on a local and global level. Parents further solidarity in their families by encouraging children to appreciate their contribution by standing in solidarity with young people of various races.

- *Care for God's Creation.* Humans are stewards of the earth, entrusted by God with this privilege. Their stewardship obliges them to honor and preserve the earth and all living things. Children need to hear this message from their earliest years and carry it forward by not wasting food and water or by similar activities.

From the beginning of the Church's life, as reflected in the New Testament and Sacred Tradition, these social principles have reminded Christians of their responsibility to serve the needy. They tell each generation that Jesus calls them to bind up the wounds of the earth, the remnants of original sin.

Seeing the poor in our families and neighborhoods and living by these seven principles of social justice afford families a wonderful agenda as they fulfill their callings as domestic churches.

Questions for Reflection

☐ What events from your past and present cause you to think more deeply about the influence of secularism today?

☐ If asked, how would you explain the Beatitudes as a blueprint for living today?

☐ How do Jesus' death and resurrection connect with our joys and sorrows and promise us new life?

☐ What events in your experience of family life helped you see more clearly that God is a God of life, not death?

☐ Why is the ultimate goal of family living directed toward the kingdom of God?

☐ What helped you appreciate that ministry to the needy enables us to better appreciate Jesus' stress on assisting the poor and underprivileged?

☐ Why is respecting the dignity of every person the groundwork upon which the other social justice principles are based?

☐ How can you encourage parents to further solidarity in their families?

Chapter Nine
The Call to Prayer and Worship

Blessed are the merciful, for they will receive mercy.

Matthew 5:7

Parents in early house churches may have done what my dad and mom did two thousand years later when they put us small children to bed at night and prayed with us. This began a habit of prayer that set the stage for our Christian Faith. From our earliest years, we learned from the Catholic climate of our home that there is more to life than what we see and do. Dad and Mom taught us that God loves us and gives us the gift of prayer to communicate with him. My earliest years reiterated the importance of a Catholic home environment.

The Acts of the Apostles mentions the first disciples in Jerusalem after Pentecost who "devoted themselves to the apostles' teaching and fellowship, to the breaking of bread and the prayers" (Acts 2:42). Like my early home experience of prayer, children of apostolic times may have learned to pray in ways similar to how my parents established an atmosphere of prayer as the foundation for our spiritual lives.

The above passage from Acts mentions four essential aspects of Christian living: teaching, fellowship, breaking of bread, and prayer. Prayer establishes the groundwork for our communication with God. Prayer was the spiritual channel that connected the disciples with the Holy Spirit and was the lifeline between them and God. The breaking of the bread refers to spiritual nourishment, especially the celebration of the Eucharist. It indicates the vital role that the Eucharistic Sacrifice played from the Church's beginning and how it reminded the disciples of Jesus' love for them and their responsibility to love one another. Fellowship shows the need for communal support and sharing love within a house church and beyond it with Christians needing support. Finally, teaching is directed to fulfilling Christ's command to go teach all nations. (Mt 28:19) This includes the call to be missionary disciples and the need to study, learn, and proclaim Jesus as Lord, while learning from the wisdom of the Holy Spirit that unlocks the mysteries of Jesus' death and resurrection. These four aspects, present in early house churches, are a skeleton for an agenda of Christian living in today's domestic church. Our Faith is grounded on implications arising from them, which we'll address.

PRAYER

St. Thérèse of Lisieux describes prayer as "a surge of the heart ... a cry of recognition and of love, embracing both trial and joy" (quoted in the *Catechism of the Catholic Church* 2558). It is a gift from God, involving a covenant and embracing communion.

When Jesus met the Samaritan woman at the well, he asked her for a drink of water. He then told her that if she knew who he was, who it was asking her for a drink, she would have asked him to give her living water, and he would have done so (see Jn 4:5–42). The *Catechism* compares this passage to the times we seek nourishment: We come seeking water from the well of God's love, and we wait as Jesus gives us himself, the living water.

Something similar happens in prayer when God comes to us, and we respond. "Prayer is the encounter of God's thirst with ours. God thirsts that we may thirst for him" (CCC 2560, referring to a quote from Saint Augustine).

The dynamic between God coming to us and our response to him in prayer is especially significant for parents when they first realize that they stand before the well of divine water as Jesus approaches and asks them for a drink of water. The water he seeks is their family's love, made in response to his love for them. What a powerful realization!

Such love goes beyond saying prayers of petition or praise in Church. Formal prayers are rooted in an overall attitude of prayer, where one's whole life becomes a prayer.

One of the first prayers that I learned was the morning offering. Reciting this prayer daily as a child set the stage for what I would do every day as I offered my life and all that it entailed to God. Such a prayer is an intentional act, embedded in us from early life and continuing as we mature. It is a foundation that enables us to turn naturally to prayer during the day as things happen, and we have to decide how to respond.

A Catholic home environment is rooted in an overall spirit of prayer that permeates the entire household and is not limited to an occasional prayer at mealtime. Parents set the tone for such a climate, one that goes a long way to establishing a vibrant domestic home church. This can be present regardless of whether both parents are Catholic. In mixed-religion households, the family climate of prayer may include aspects of different faiths that mutually complement each other and lead to a more ecumenical flavor that permeates the home.

BREAKING OF THE BREAD

Breaking of the bread is the second aspect of Christian living. In the New Testament, it includes sharing a common meal and the Eucharist. Referring to the early disciples after Pentecost, the Acts of the Apostles says, "They broke bread at home and ate their food with glad and generous hearts, praising God and having the goodwill of all the people" (Acts 2:46–47).

To show their unity and need for community, early Christians often ate a meal together, as indicated in the road to Emmaus story, where after walking the road with two of his disciples, Jesus stayed with them for dinner. Luke's Gospel says, "When he was at the table with them, he took bread, blessed and broke it, and gave it to them" (Lk 24:30).

The disciples, previously unaware that they were walking with Jesus, recognized him when he broke the bread. This was more than an ordinary act; the disciples saw it in light of the Last Supper, when Jesus broke bread, changed it into his body, and gave it to them.

What the early Christian households did as they came together to break bread serves as a reminder that effective communication often happens when we eat together. Business associates faced with challenging issues often discuss such matters over a meal. The same applies to friends or a family going out for dinner. There is something lasting about sharing one's hopes and concerns over a meal. How appropriate that in this act of eating together, Christians become one with Jesus and one another!

I discovered this oneness with family members during the

2020 pandemic. When we could not get together in person, we found comfort by arranging our Sunday evening meals so that we could eat together on Zoom. It reminded us of beautiful family gatherings on Sundays while growing up.

Breaking bread is symbolic of spending time together as a Christian family. Its connection with the Eucharist reminds us that we eat for more than survival. In the Eucharist, Jesus is the powerful binding force, keeping a family together in good and difficult times. Connecting with one another in the Eucharist is a grace-filled way to remain united in a family, united with Christ, and joined with other believers in the Christian community.

For this reason, Christian domestic churches, led by parents, need to recognize the value of eating together. It is far more than a time to say a simple prayer before meals. Rather, it serves as a powerful reminder that the mutual sharing that takes place at a meal brings families closer together and is a steppingstone for the spiritual nourishment that comes in the Eucharist. Every meal becomes a prayer when families give thanks for the continued presence of the Lord in their homes.

Besides reminding us of the significance of eating together, the breaking of bread also leads us to the Eucharist and indicates its importance in the Christian life. Saint Paul's First Letter to the Corinthians recalls its institution with the words, "The Lord Jesus on the night when he was betrayed took a loaf of bread, and when he had given thanks, he broke it and said, 'This is my body that is for you'" (1 Cor 11:23–24).

Early Christians centered their gatherings around the Eucharist. As they assembled on Sunday, the day of the Lord, they initially nourished their bodies and spirits with food and drink at an agape meal and then later celebrated the Eucharist. After abuses coming from eating or drinking too much crept into their celebrations, the Sunday gathering of Christians in house churches were limited to celebrating the Eucharist, as the believers broke bread and drank of the cup to celebrate the dying and rising of the Lord.

FELLOWSHIP

Fellowship is the third aspect of Christian living. Early Christian households centered their fellowship on Jesus. They expected his imminent return in glory at the end of the world. This provided the motivation for their communal lifestyle and shared values, beliefs, and possessions. They recognized themselves as members of God's household and shared what they had with one another. As Paul says to the Ephesians, "So then you are no longer strangers and aliens, but you are citizens with the saints and also members of the household of God, built upon the foundation of the apostles and prophets, with Christ Jesus himself as the cornerstone" (Eph 2:19–20).

Beset with persecution from the Romans and problems with unsympathetic Roman citizens, early house churches were nonetheless the focus of Christian growth. They provided the hope necessary to sustain Jesus' followers during persecution. Their energy came from believers praying together in the temple and in their homes. Centered on Jesus, Christians were people of prayer. It was their communication channel, keeping them in touch with God and one another.

Contemporary society differs from what they encountered. They experienced persecution and death; our culture trends toward lukewarmness and superficiality. Today's culture may be more challenging than what the first Christians faced. Persecution led early Christians to deep commitment to their Faith; our culture often moves Christians to apathy and disbelief. In the long run, which is more challenging? Regardless of our answer, modern domestic churches can take solace from the realization that a firm commitment, like the early Christians made, is a prerequisite for our homes to become vibrant witnesses to Christ.

When reflecting on early and contemporary fellowship, we recognize that different kinds of fellowship exist. On the one hand, employees of business organizations may get together to celebrate success in obtaining a new contract. This involves fellowship arising from achieving a functional goal. In some homes, this type of functional fellowship predominates, as parents and children go their separate ways, leaving little time for the family to spend together in deeper fellowship.

In contrast, there is a deeper kind of fellowship which centers around care, compassion, and other ultimate life dimensions. It includes genuine dialogue, which sets the stage for deep interpersonal fellowship and grounds the prayer life of family members. This happened in early house churches and still occurs today.

This more ultimate type of fellowship becomes Christian prayer if it is centered on Christ. When this happens, it becomes evident why we need each other, first to fulfill our human needs and second to fulfill our deep spiritual need for meaning. These go beyond the functional and focus on God as the center of our being.

Love, manifested in deep fellowship, becomes a powerful prayer when Jesus is at its center. Saint Paul alludes to the union of fellowship and prayer when he says, "I pray that, according to the riches of his glory, he may grant that you may be strengthened in your inner being with power through his Spirit, and that Christ may dwell in your hearts through faith, as you are being rooted and grounded in love" (Eph 3:16–17).

TEACHING

Teaching is the fourth aspect of Christian living. We recognize its importance as we learn new things from others. Human growth happens when we use our reason and learn from teachers in the fields of technology, history, religion, and more. Learning these things teaches us how to live in an ever-changing world. While other animals depend largely on habit or instinct to live, humans are guided by their reason and will, assisted by what others teach them.

Experiences of love and trust are deep modes of learning, often taught by our parents, friends, siblings, and others through relationships involving love, care, and compassion. We learn from others how to get along in this world and how to connect to deep levels of faith as missionary disciples. Most of our attitudes toward religious and secular matters are learned in the family.

Even when a person is self-taught, this happens because someone put him or her on the right path of learning. Put simply, we need one another, and community is essential. In the context of faith, this is manifested most fully when Jesus comes to us and guides our Christian living. Then, we better understand and appreciate the great mysteries of our Faith. This movement to conversion begins with — and continues in — prayer to God, our supreme teacher, as we recall Jesus' disciples asking him, "Lord, teach us to pray." He responded with the greatest prayer, the Our Father (see Lk 11:1–4). May we do as he taught us and offer this prayer to the Father!

The deepest learning occurs in prayer, often in meditation and silent worship. Here God teaches us. In prayer, we invite Jesus, the master teacher, to come and teach us that God is with us, encouraging us to direct our actions by what we learn in prayer. With prayer, life becomes a vibrant profession of the meaning of our lives. Without it, life is a series of passing events, not a beautiful mosaic interwoven with God's wisdom and directed beyond this life to eternity.

Grounded in prayer, we teach others as we have been taught. This begins in earliest childhood with simple acts such as brushing our teeth or getting dressed. As we grow, we build layer upon layer of our understanding, influenced by what we have learned.

This continues as we learn to act for ourselves and modify the teaching we have learned. Viewed in this way, it is easier to understand the vital role of the teacher, beginning with our parents and extending to school, church, technology, and other learning environments.

Learning what Jesus taught his disciples was central in the early Church. A top priority of Jesus' followers was to learn and live by authentic, orthodox teaching. The early Church needed to get correct what Jesus taught. For this reason, when Christians went astray, witnessed in the Letter of Saint Paul to Timothy, Church leaders quickly reminded them to be faithful to Jesus' teaching. Paul says, "I urge you … to remain in Ephesus so that you may instruct certain people not to teach any different doctrine, and not to occupy themselves with myths and endless genealogies that promote speculations rather than the divine training that is known by faith" (1 Tm 1:3–4).

The Church's hierarchy is mindful of this injunction, as it oversees the teaching of Church doctrine. To ensure faithfulness to what Jesus taught, Christian parents teach their children simply and clearly the truths that the Church instructs them to teach.

Questions for Reflection

❑ Why is it important for a pastor or parish team to encourage families to establish an atmosphere of prayer in their home?

❑ Why is breaking of the bread an apt symbol of healthy family living as it relates to the Eucharist?

❑ Discuss: Without prayer, life becomes a series of events, not a beautiful mosaic interwoven with God's wisdom and directed beyond this life to eternity.

❑ Why is it essential for pastors and others in parish ministry to stress the need for parents to teach their children the essentials of the Faith?

Chapter Ten

The Call to Faith Formation

Blessed are the pure in heart, for they will see God.

Matthew 5:8

The processes of faith formation today and for the first Christians contain similar elements. At their center is the reality that faith grows and becomes stronger if we faithfully follow the promptings of the Holy Spirit, adhere to the teachings of the Beatitudes and God's commandment of love, and celebrate the Lord's continued presence in the broader parish community, especially in the Eucharist.

The climate of the first house churches was vital for prayer and support, as is the climate of our homes today. Here we learn to pray and receive wisdom to face the blessings and temptations of the secular world. As with the first disciples, a family's growth in faith varies from family to family, reflected in the following stories:

Ellie and Mark asked me to officiate at their wedding. I knew Ellie for several years before she married. It was a joke in her family that she would never marry, because she was too picky about a spouse. None of the guys she dated had suited her. One of her chief criteria for a marriage partner was his adherence to the Catholic Faith. Once she said, "If I am going to marry for life and be happy, I want my family to reflect the Catholic beliefs that I have been taught at home. My future spouse's attitudes and values must be in tune with mine; otherwise I will not be happy and will not fulfill my vocation as a committed Catholic." I could not argue with her logic.

I encouraged Ellie to keep trying to find the man that would make her happy. This went on for several years. Then, one day Ellie called and said, "Father Bob, I found the man I am looking for. His name is Mark, and I'd like you to meet him." This we did, and eventually they married. Her search paid off. Today, Ellie, Mark, and their four children are a wonderful family.

Sean and Abby's story is different. Sean is Presbyterian, and Abby is Catholic. Over time, I counseled them and got to know them quite well. They were like-minded in their belief in Jesus and many Church teachings. After they married, they developed a beautiful ecumenical family. Their family too was a domestic church.

What does the growth in love and faith of these couples tell us about family faith formation? First, it indicates that faith formation is a process, and for a married couple and their family, their secular and religious cultures are very influential. The two couples described above manifested this in how they worked out their family faith responsibilities in a busy world. Second, faith formation is rooted in God's presence in their lives. Third, it is influenced by their relationships and working together as a couple to create a Christian climate in their home. Fourth, since faith extends outside of the family, it is necessary to reach out beyond the family and find a parish that supports and encourages faith growth. Fifth, the faith formation process changes and shifts with each family, for every family is different.

ASPECTS OF FAITH FORMATION

With these five elements in mind, remember that effective faith formation centers on the climate of the home. This establishes the foundation for the entire process. Within it, virtuous living is the goal.

The need for virtuous living is reflected in the Second Letter of Saint Peter. In speaking to an early Christian community, he says, "You must make every effort to support your faith with goodness, and goodness with knowledge, and knowledge with self-control, and self-control with endurance, and endurance with godliness, and godliness with mutual affection, and mutual affection with love" (1:5–7). Motivated by the Beatitudes, these words indicate that there are necessary requirements for any process of faith formation. They enable us to look more deeply into a family's growth in faith. Put simply, they involve information, formation, and transformation.

Information

From early childhood, infants learn many things as they constantly reach out beyond themselves, witnessed in their hand and bodily movements. The built-in need to assimilate new facts is nature's prerequisite to coping with various situations and life circumstances.

As children grow, what they learn helps them get along in the world. The need to learn is not limited to learning about the physical universe. It also is the foundation for a person's psychological and spiritual growth. For believers, interaction with the world around them, beginning with their parents and siblings, sets the foundation for establishing core values necessary to live a moral life.

Humans, however, cannot know all there is about life from what they learn by reason alone. God revealed in the Scriptures what he wants us to know about the deeper recesses of life's mysteries. This Revelation reached its climax in the person of Jesus Christ. He taught us what is necessary for a happy life here and eternal life hereafter. Central to his teachings are the Beatitudes, the blueprints for Christian living.

Knowledge of the Beatitudes helps us better appreciate the context, meaning, and implications of what Jesus taught. As a formula for Christian living, each Beatitude has deep biblical roots and tells us how to live a good life. As we acquire spiritual information from the Beatitudes, Scripture, and basic Church teaching, our learning affects us and becomes a part of our faith formation.

Learning happens in many ways. From early years, parents teach their children how to hold a fork or how to throw a ball. We get information from daily living. We put on our coat when the weather is cold outside or wear sunglasses to protect our eyes on sunny days. Such intentional learning begins in the family, as children watch their parents and strive to imitate them.

Intentional learning takes place at home and as we go to school. It happens when we read on our own, watch television, listen to the radio, use the computer, listen to others, and work on the internet. We intentionally learn to grow and prosper in our fact-oriented society. Much intentional learning is also intellectual learning.

It is easy to forget, however, that intellectual learning is not the only kind of information we acquire. Western civilization concentrates on this mode of knowing. From it has sprung the vast scientific and technological society of the twenty-first century. In addition, other modes of learning exist, evidenced in the lives of earlier peoples and Eastern cultures that stress the significance of intuitive learning.

Besides the modes of learning indicated above, many kinds of learning are of a spiritual nature, revealed by God in Scripture and Sacred Tradition. We believe revealed teaching as a matter of faith, for Divine Revelation is beyond human analysis. Examples include the belief that there are two natures in Jesus (human and divine) and the Trinitarian belief that there are three divine persons in one God.

From faith, we learn that revealed truths are the basis of Catholic belief and practice. These truths are taught to children first by their parents and later in parish schools of religion, in catechetical classes at Catholic schools, in RCIA sessions, and from the pulpit at Mass. This information is essential for vibrant Catholic living.

Formation

Culture is a powerful formative aspect of life. What we assimilate from our culture and internalize subconsciously sets the foundation for our attitudes and actions. For instance, many values and priorities of a child reared in a religious home, where parents regularly pray and attend church, differ from those of a child whose parents do not profess any religious belief. A peer group, influential friend, or relative has a significant influence on the physical, psychological, and spiritual formation of a child or teenager. The depictions of violence and sexual promiscuity promoted by the internet, media, and television have a powerful negative influence on value formation.

Formation goes beyond intellectual knowledge and the assimilation of facts. A person can know intellectually what is right or wrong, but this does not mean that this knowledge convinces him or her to act upon this knowledge or that it significantly affects one's behavior. A teenager can be an "*A* student" and leave much to be desired regarding moral conduct. An adult can know the teachings of the Faith but act in a contrary way.

For knowledge to make a difference, it must be internalized, personalized, and made one's own. This requires formation of the whole person — body, soul, and spirit — and includes the sensory, emotional, and spiritual components of who we are.

The *Directory for Catechesis* addresses the all-encompassing dimension of formation when it says, "*Formation* is an ongoing process that, under the guidance of the Spirit and in the living womb of the Christian community, helps the baptized person to *take shape*, which means unveiling his deepest identity which is that of being a son [or daughter] of God in profound communion with his [or her] brothers [and sisters]."[1] The *Directory* emphasizes that formation involves a transformation of the person.

Transformation

While engaged in a formation process, a time comes when we get it. This happens when what we learn is internalized, and we respond accordingly. This is an "*aha* moment." The formation process for a Christian involves the internalization of a value, more specifically the evangelical message, so that it can serve as a guide for one's mission and role in the Christian community.[2] This transformative moment leads to a change of attitude and action, reflected in Saint Paul's Letter to the Colossians: "As God's chosen ones, holy and beloved, clothe yourselves with compassion, kindness, humility, meekness, and patience" (Col 3:12). These words remind us of Jesus' words that we are the "light of the world" (Mt 5:14).

If learning does not involve more than the assimilation of facts, then words — such as the Scripture above — simply convey *information* that we may not internalize. To take a step further, we need to reflect on the words and believe that we are the "light of the world," appreciating that we can make a difference in our homes, schools, and neighborhoods. In so doing, we engage in a process of *formation*, often aided by prayer, discussion, or conversation with friends. In addition, one more step is necessary for spiritual growth; namely, *transformation*. At this stage, we believe that we are the "light of the world" (Mt 5:14), and this leads us to action. Such knowledge and belief transform who we are, as awareness that we are the "light of the world" moves us to "go therefore and make disciples of all nations" (Mt 28:19), a transformation that changes us into missionary disciples.

MINISTRIES INFLUENCING FAITH FORMATION

Catholic evangelization is the goal of missionary discipleship. In early house churches, Jesus' disciples were convinced that they were to share his Good News. Proclaiming the kingdom of God was Jesus' mission, which he turned over to his disciples when he ascended into heaven.

Imagine how the disciples reacted when they were convinced that their top priority was to be missionary disciples! Reflecting on their response to Jesus' call still motivates Jesus' followers today to do the same. What would the Church be like if parents taught their children from infancy onward that they are disciples of Jesus with his mission motivating their mission?

For this to happen, three chief aspects of ministry enable the evangelization process to occur. These are the ministries of Word, worship, and service. We consider each of them. The ministry of the Word includes catechesis, preaching, and religious instruction and formation. These take place in parish ministries such as the RCIA, catechetical sessions, and Catholic school programs. They begin, however, in the home, where parents and their family delve into the word of God in informal and formal ways. This is vitally important, for the *Directory for Catechesis* says, "Believing parents, with their daily example of life, have the most effective capacity to transmit the beauty of the Christian faith to their children."[3]

Such informal testimony sets the stage for formal or systematic catechesis by parents, catechists, and liturgical activities. The *Directory for Catechesis*, quoting *Amoris Laetitia*, says, "'The Church is called to cooperate with parents through suitable pastoral initiatives, assisting them in the fulfillment of their educational mission' to become above all the first catechists of their own children."[4]

Because catechesis is intimately tied to the proclamation of the Word and is a chief aspect of the evangelization process, it is imperative that parents include it in their efforts to develop a first-class faith formation process for their children. Pastors are encouraged to do all they can to support this endeavor.

The ministry of worship, including prayer, centers around the Mass and sacraments. Usually, these take place in parish settings, where sacred rituals are fostered and a desire to participate in them grows. They begin in the home in the prayers and rituals that children learn in their family.

The ministry of service involves all service activities directed to the kingdom of God. They include social justice initiatives of a communal and individual kind. The strongest motivation to practice them often comes from the family and a person's decision to serve the poor and needy. The domestic church plays a vital role in making these ministries an integral part of Christian family living.

Faith formation in the home happens in the relationship between family and parish, with the outside culture having a strong influence on this process. The challenge for parishes is to connect the unchangeable truths of faith with the special needs of families. This is accomplished when good connections exist between a family and the parish. In some cases, this also includes a relationship with a Catholic school.

Faith formation happening in the home is vital, for the family unit is the most significant place where information, formation, and transformation happen. This was the case in Jesus' life, as he was formed in the Jewish tradition by his parents. In a similar way, Catholic parents can do the same in the Catholic climate of their homes.

The Catholic climate in the home develops in multiple ways, with the parents playing a central role. Preparation for family faith begins from the start of a serious relationship between a man and a woman prior to marriage. This sets the stage for the eventual development of a Catholic family climate and its influence on the Catholic spirit of their home.

Family life centers around the parents. Consequently, from their engagement onwards, a couple's continued spiritual growth sets the stage for receiving the graces which carry their family through good and bad times and prepare family members to appreciate their roles as missionary disciples.

After marriage, the role of the parents in faith formation becomes more direct, especially when children come. Parental influence, more than any other factor, plays a vital role in developing a Catholic spirit in the home. How this happens is different in every family, for the formation of family members is influenced by their relationships.

Family faith, influenced by parental attitudes toward faith, happens in an ongoing way through prayer, family catechesis, and speaking about God and Catholic matters. This lasts throughout the life of the family and is especially important in early years. Family faith formation is a process, strongly influenced by the connection a family has with the parish. The domestic church unites with the parish church and the larger Catholic community to grow, learn, and receive support through the sacraments, especially the Eucharist.

In this process, the sacraments are vitally important. In their own way, they influence the family and larger Catholic community. Sacramental events, such as a child's first Communion, are times when faith can leap forward, as new directions emerge.

The sacraments, especially the Mass, are wonderful occasions for families to give thanks for their relationships and to examine the love they have for one another. In this regard, the *Directory for Catechesis* addresses the family's importance when it says, "The family is a community of love and of life, made up of 'a complex of interpersonal relationships … — married life, fatherhood and motherhood, filiation and fraternity — through which each human person is introduced into the "human family" and into the "family of God," which is the Church.'"[5]

Faith formation, rooted in the Eucharist, is a vital aspect of every domestic church. It begins in the home and leads to the Eucharist, and after celebrating with the parish community, domestic churches return home to live their lives in the spirit of Christ. In this process, Archbishop José Gomez offers a fitting conclusion to this chapter on faith formation. He says:

> The first Christians evangelized by the way they lived. And the way they lived was to be in this world but not of this world. They lived the same lives as their neighbors, but in a different way … The first Christian families changed the world — simply by living the teachings of Jesus and his Church. And my friends, we can change the world again, by following the same path.[6]

Questions for Reflection

❑ Why does an effective process of Catholic faith formation center on the climate of the home?

❑ Discuss: God reveals in Scripture what he wants us to know about the deep recesses of life's mystery.

❑ Why do pastors and other parish leaders need to stress that catechesis is an essential aspect of the faith formation process?

❑ Discuss the implications of the following statement for pastors and parish staffs: "The formation process for a Christian involves the internalization of a value, more specifically the evangelical message … as a guide for one's mission."[7]

Conclusion

Families are people of hope, so long as they maintain confidence in the love of God who promises them new life, witnessed by Jesus' resurrection. During their joys and sorrows, trust in God is their response as missionary disciples. To the degree that they manifest their continued hope they grow in love, wisdom, and knowledge.

Christian missionary discipleship is a vocation to which we as family members are called. With Mary the Mother of God as our model, we strive to imitate her life of love and compassion, while forming our families into domestic churches. Keeping our call to missionary discipleship in mind, we conclude with words from the *Directory for Catechesis*:

Ensuring a domestic atmosphere of humility, tenderness, contemplation, and concern for others, Mary educated Jesus, the Word made flesh, in the way of justice and obedience to the will of the Father. In turn, the Mother learned to follow the Son, becoming the first and the most perfect of his disciples. On the morning of Pentecost, the Mother of the Church presided with her prayer over the beginning of evangelization, under the action of the Holy Spirit, and today she continues to intercede so that the people of the present time may encounter Christ and, through faith in him, be saved by receiving in fullness the life of the children of God.[1]

May these words of hope bless Christian families who follow Jesus in our challenging world!

Acknowledgments

The following acknowledgments are made for words used in this book, taken from my work previously published in other books and magazines. Excerpts and summaries of these works are included here with permission of the publishers who previously published them.

REV. ROBERT J. HATER'S PREVIOUSLY PUBLISHED SOURCES

- Materials used in this book from chapter two, section 1 taken from *Your [Imperfect] Holy Family: See the Good, Make it Better* (Cincinnati, Ohio: Franciscan Media, 2015).

- Materials used in this book from chapter two, section 2a taken from *The Priest* magazine (Huntington, Indiana: Our Sunday Visitor, 2020).

OTHER SOURCES

- Archbishop José Gomez, keynote address for the Conference on Liturgy and the Domestic Church, University of Notre Dame, June 2019, quoted in "Families are a radical witness to hope in modern society, Archbishop Gomez says," Catholic News Agency, June 19, 2019, https://www.catholicnewsagency.com/news/41584/families-are-a-radical-witness-to-hope-in-modern-society-archbishop-gomez-says.

- Biblical passages taken from the *New Revised Standard Version Bible: Catholic Edition.*

- Materials in Church documents quoted from publications of the United States Conference of Catholic Bishops.

- Further information on the domestic church can be found in Charisse D. Rubio's master's degree thesis, "Ecclesiology of the Domestic Church: History and Implications" (Athenaeum of Ohio, 2020).

Notes

FOREWORD

1. Francis, *Evangelii Gaudium*, November 24, 2013, Vatican.va, par. 28.

2. Francis, *Amoris Laetitia*, March 19, 2016, Vatican.va, par. 139.

PART ONE: SETTING THE FOUNDATION

1. Francis, *AL,* par. 11.

2. Second Vatican Council, *Lumen Gentium,* November 21, 1964, Vatican.va, par. 11.

3. Pontifical Council for the Promotion of the New Evangelization, *Directory for Catechesis: New Edition* (United States Conference of Catholic Bishops, June 25, 2020), 180; cf. Paul VI, *Apostolicam Actuositatem*, November 18, 1965, Vatican.va, par. 10.

4. Pontifical Council for the Promotion of the New Evangelization, *Directory for Catechesis*, 179.

5. This section is based on my article, "Why Building the Domes-

tic Church Matters," *The Priest* magazine, August 2019, https://www
.thepriest.com/2019/08/15/why-building-the-domestic-church-matters/.

6. John Paul II, *Gratissimam Sane*, February 2, 1994, Vatican.va, par. 1.

7. Francis, *AL*, par. 202.

CHAPTER ONE: MADE NOT BORN

1. Francis, *AL*, par. 276.

2. Tertullian, *Apology*, par. 28.

3. Congregation for the Clergy, *General Directory for Catechesis*, August 11, 1997, Vatican.va, par. 255.

4. Archbishop José Gomez, keynote address for the Conference on Liturgy and the Domestic Church, University of Notre Dame, June 2019, quoted in "Families are a radical witness to hope in modern society, Archbishop Gomez says," Catholic News Agency, June 19, 2019, https://www.catholicnewsagency.com/news/41584/families-are-a-radical-witness-to-hope-in-modern-society-archbishop-gomez-says.

5. Congregation for the Clergy, "The pastoral conversion of the Parish community in the service of the evangelising mission of the Church," July 20, 2020, Press.vatican.va.

CHAPTER TWO: TODAY'S FAMILIES IN LIGHT OF THE PAST

1. Francis, *AL*, par. 30.

2. The material from this section is taken largely from my book, *Your [Imperfect] Holy Family: See the Good, Make It Better* (Cincinnati, Ohio: Franciscan Media, 2015). Reprinted here with permission.

3. Synod of Bishops, III Extraordinary General Assembly, *The Pastoral Challenges of the Family in the Context of Evangelization*, June 26, 2014, Vatican.va, par. 36.

4. This section is adapted from my article, "Why Building the

Domestic Church Matters," *The Priest* magazine, https://www
.thepriest.com/2019/08/15/why-building-the-domestic-church
-matters/

5. Francis, *AL,* par. 136.

CHAPTER THREE: NEW DIRECTIONS IN FAMILY MINISTRY

1. Francis, *AL,* par. 139.

2. For further reference on the domestic church, see Charisse D.
Rubio, "Ecclesiology of the Domestic Church: History and Implications" (master's thesis, Athenaeum of Ohio, 2020), https://etd.
ohiolink.edu/apexprod/rws_etd/send_file/send
?accession=athe159223336608125&disposition=inline.

3. Saint Augustine, *Tractates on the Gospel of John*, tractate 51,
par. 13, trans. John Gibb, *Nicene and Post-Nicene Fathers, First Series,*
Vol. 7 (Buffalo, New York: Christian Literature Publishing Co., 1888),
ed. Kevin Knight, *New Advent,* 2005, https://www.newadvent .org/fa-
thers/1701051.htm.

4. Second Vatican Council, *Gaudium et Spes*, December 7, 1965,
Vatican.va, par. 48.

5. Second Vatican Council, *LG,* par. 9.

6. Ibid., par. 11.

7. Paul VI, *Evangelii Nuntiandi,* December 8, 1975, Vatican.va, par.
71.

8. John Paul II, *Familiaris Consortio*, November 22, 1981, Vatican.
va, par. 17–18.

9. Ibid., par. 39.

10. Ibid., par. 50.

11. Ibid.

12. John Paul II, *Christifideles Laici*, December 30, 1988, Vatican.
va, par.14.

13. John Paul II, *CL,* par. 62.

14. Benedict XVI, "The Prayer and the Holy Family of Nazareth,"

December 28, 2011, Vatican.va.

15. National Conference of Catholic Bishops, *A Family Perspective in Church and Society: Committee on Marriage and Family*, Tenth Anniversary Edition (Washington, DC: USCCB Publishing, 1998), 7.

16. Francis, *EG*, par. 67.

17. Ibid., par. 120.

18. Francis, *AL*, par. 30.

19. Ibid., par. 136.

20. Ibid., par. 136–137.

21. Ibid., par. 200.

22. Pontifical Council for the Promotion of the New Evangelization, 39-41.

23. Ibid., 228-230.

24. Ibid., 36.

CHAPTER FOUR: CULTURE, CLIMATE, AND THE DOMESTIC CHURCH

1. Pontifical Council for the Promotion of the New Evangelization, 36.

2. George H. Litwin and Robert A. Stringer, *Motivation and Organizational Climate* (Harvard Business School, Division of Research, 1968).

3. Francis, *AL*, par. 90.

4. Gordon Willard Allport, *The Individual and His Religion: A Psychological Interpretation* (New York: Macmillan Pub Company, 1967).

PART TWO: FORMING DOMESTIC CHURCHES

1. This story appears in my book *Your [Imperfect] Holy Family: See the Good, Make it Better.*

CHAPTER FIVE: THE CALL TO RELATIONSHIP

1. Francis, *AL*, par. 57.

CHAPTER SIX: THE CALL TO ACCOUNTABILITY, HOSPITALITY, AND EVANGELIZATION

1. Pontifical Council for the Promotion of the New Evangelization, 28.

2. Ibid., 32; cf. Revelation 21:5.

3. Ibid., 33.

4. Ibid., 36-37.

5. Ibid., 36.

CHAPTER SEVEN: THE CALL TO MISSIONARY DISCIPLESHIP

1. Francis, *AL,* par. 201.

2. Francis, *EG,* par. 19.

3. Pontifical Council for the Promotion of the New Evangelization, 29.

4. Ibid.

5. Second Vatican Council, *Ad Gentes,* December 7, 1965, Vatican.va.

6. Francis, "Sunday Angelus," July 15, 2018, Vatican.va.

7. Pontifical Council for the Promotion of the New Evangelization, 104.

8. Ibid.

CHAPTER EIGHT: THE CALL TO THE KINGDOM OF JUSTICE AND PEACE

1. Archbishop José Gomez, 2019.

2. Francis, *AL,* par. 11.

3. Francis, *AL,* par. 16.

4. These principles are taken from the United States Conference of Catholic Bishops as outlined in the documents *Sharing Catholic Social Teaching: Challenges and Directions* (Washington, D.C.: USCB Publishing, 1998) and *Forming Consciences for Faithful Citizen-*

ship: A Call to Political Responsibility (Washington, D.C.: USCCB Publishing, 2015).

CHAPTER NINE: THE CALL TO PRAYER AND WORSHIP

1. Pontifical Council for the Promotion of the New Evangelization, 85.
2. Ibid.
3. Ibid., 81.
4. Ibid.
5. Ibid., 137, quoting *Familiaris Consortio.*
6. Archbishop José Gomez, 2019.
7. Pontifical Council for the Promotion of the New Evangelization, 85.

CHAPTER TEN: THE CALL TO FAITH FORMATION

1. Pontifical Council for the Promotion of the New Evangelization, 251.

About the Author

Fr. Robert J. Hater, PhD, was ordained a priest of the Archdiocese of Cincinnati in 1959. He is a Professor Emeritus at the University of Dayton and a retired Professor of Systematic and Pastoral Theology and founder of the Adult Spirituality Institute at the Athenaeum of Ohio. He earned his PhD in Philosophy from St. John's University (NY). Previously, he has served as an archdiocesan religious education director, university professor, associate pastor, and high school teacher/counselor. He has lectured internationally on the topics of ministry, evangelization, spirituality, and catechesis. He is the author of about three dozen books and hundreds of articles.

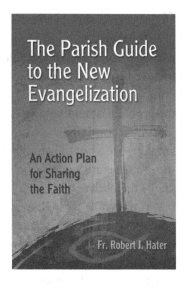

You might also like:

Renewing Catholic Family Life: Experts Explore New Directions in Family Spirituality and Family Ministry
By Gregory K. Popcak, PhD

Acollection of essays from the Catholic Family Life Symposium in July 2019 sponsored by OSV Institute and held at the University of Notre Dame brings together internationally recognized theologians, social scientists, and pastoral ministry professionals to explore the renewal of Catholic family life.

Readers will discover not only the challenges facing faithful families, but practical, empirically-based responses to those challenges.

RENEWING CATHOLIC FAMILY LIFE

Experts Explore New Directions in
Family Spirituality and Family Ministry

The Catholic Family Life Symposium
University of Notre Dame – July 18-21, 2019
Gregory K. Popcak, PhD – Editor

(OSV) INSTITUTE

NATIONAL
REACH.
PERSONAL
IMPACT.

Available at
OSVCatholicBookstore.com
or wherever books are sold